# Remembering the Body

# Remembering the Body

*Preaching that Affirms Sexuality*

SARAH TRAVIS

CASCADE *Books* · Eugene, Oregon

REMEMBERING THE BODY
Preaching that Affirms Sexuality

Copyright © 2025 Sarah Travis. All rights reserved. Except for brief quotations in critical publications or reviews, no part of this book may be reproduced in any manner without prior written permission from the publisher. Write: Permissions, Wipf and Stock Publishers, 199 W. 8th Ave., Suite 3, Eugene, OR 97401.

Cascade Books
An Imprint of Wipf and Stock Publishers
199 W. 8th Ave., Suite 3
Eugene, OR 97401

www.wipfandstock.com

PAPERBACK ISBN: 978-1-6667-7669-0
HARDCOVER ISBN: 978-1-6667-7670-6
EBOOK ISBN: 978-1-6667-7671-3

*Cataloguing-in-Publication data:*

Names: Travis, Sarah, author.

Title: Remembering the body : preaching that affirms sexuality / Sarah Travis.

Description: Eugene, OR: Cascade Books, 2025 | Includes bibliographical references.

Identifiers: ISBN 978-1-6667-7669-0 (paperback) | ISBN 978-1-6667-7670-6 (hardcover) | ISBN 978-1-6667-7671-3 (ebook)
Subjects: LCSH: Human body—Religious aspects—Christianity. | Homosexuality—Religious aspects—Christianity. | Preaching.
Classification: BR115.H6 T73 2025 (paperback) | BR115.H6 (ebook)

03/14/25

For my daughters.

# Contents

| | | |
|---|---|---|
| *Acknowledgments* | | ix |
| Introduction | | 1 |
| | A Wounded Body | 1 |
| | Defining Terms and Assumptions | 3 |
| | Finding My Voice | 5 |
| | Preaching and Sexuality | 9 |
| | Remembering the Body | 12 |
| 1 | Preaching and the Body | 17 |
| | Embodied Beings | 17 |
| | Centering Bodies in the Pulpit | 22 |
| | Stumbling Blocks to Preaching About Sexuality | 27 |
| | Trauma and Grief | 29 |
| | Healing Wounds | 33 |
| 2 | The Body of Christ | 35 |
| | Coming to Terms with Christ's Body | 35 |
| | A Wounded Community | 39 |
| | Preaching and the Care of the Body | 44 |
| | Remembering Our Baptisms: The Memory of Love's Refrain | 45 |
| | Baptismal Identity and Connection | 47 |
| | Broken Body, Broken Promises | 48 |
| | The Baptized Body | 50 |

## Contents

| | | |
|---|---|---|
| 3 | Preaching That Weeps, Confesses, and Resists | 52 |
| | Remembering Rightly | 52 |
| | Preaching as Weeping and Confession | 54 |
| | Confessing the Harm | 57 |
| | Assurance of Pardon | 62 |
| | Preaching as Resistance | 63 |
| | Encountering Opposition | 68 |
| 4 | Preaching a Gospel of Reconciliation | 70 |
| | Untangling Gospel | 70 |
| | Safe Space and Reconciliation | 74 |
| | Unity and Forgiveness | 77 |
| | Strengthening Connective Tissues | 81 |
| | Healing Wounds | 84 |
| 5 | Healing Biblical Interpretation | 86 |
| | Difficult Questions | 86 |
| | Biblical Interpretation that Re-Members the Body of Christ | 93 |
| | Queer Biblical Hermeneutics | 96 |
| | Affirming Biblical Interpretation | 99 |
| 6 | Affirming Preaching: Sermons That Remember | 106 |
| | Good News, Bad News | 106 |
| | Protecting the Body | 110 |
| | Hospitality | 114 |
| | Belonging and Identity | 118 |
| | Healing the Body | 119 |
| | The Art of Remembering | 121 |
| 7 | Sermons That Affirm | 124 |
| | My House Will Be Called a House of Prayer for Everyone | 124 |
| | The Wideness of God's Mercy | 129 |
| | What's in a Name? | 134 |
| *Bibliography* | | 139 |

# Acknowledgments

As I write this, dark clouds gather in the political realm in North America. There is a rising tide of suspicion and hatred against the LGBTQ community. I am afraid for my companions on the road who identify as queer. The journey ahead will require courage and compassion in equal measure. This book is a drop in the bucket, one thread of a conversation that has global implications for the body of Christ. In many ways it is a penitential project, undertaken as a means of assuaging my guilt over my own silence, and on behalf of a church that I perceive to have failed in its care of its own body. It is an invitation to confession, and an invitation to receive the wholehearted forgiveness of the Holy One. It is not too late for the church to repent and heal.

This project was inspired by a series of conversations which took place at Knox College, University of Toronto in the fall of 2022. I am grateful for those who have been willing to be vulnerable and fight for justice and equity in my institution, particularly principal Ernest van Eck, dean Christine Mitchell, registrar Shawn Stovell, professor emeritus Charles Fensham, and MDiv student Linda Endicott. Linda, Charles, and Shawn each read the manuscript, providing generous and thought-provoking feedback which is reflected in these pages.

I owe a debt of gratitude to the congregation of Norval Presbyterian Church, whose generosity allowed me the time and space to think through this project, and eventually bring it to life. I have absolute trust in my wonderful copy editor Lianne Biggar, and any errors that remain are my own. Finally, thank you to my

## Acknowledgments

husband Paul Miller and to my children. It is a delight to watch as you discover your own identities. You are loved just as you are.

Epiphany, 2023

# Introduction

## A WOUNDED BODY

THE BODY OF CHRIST is broken. Christian debates about sexual diversity have bruised and wounded the body of the church. Some of these wounds and fractures are fresh and recent; others are decades, even centuries old. There has been exclusion, persecution, hatred, and erasure. As much as harm has been focused on LGBTQ individuals, the whole community has suffered. This is what it is to live as the body of Christ—when one suffers, we all suffer. As the body of Christ has been dismembered by hatred, so it must be re-membered. This book is an attempt to name the harm and imagine healing through the preaching of the church. Weaving theology with lived experience, I propose a progressive vision for preaching sexuality in the church today. This is primarily a task of remembering, literally knitting the body of the church back together. As much as this is a task of healing and repairing relationships, it is also about remembering who we are as God's children and the implications of this holy identity for all our relationships.

As often as the church has failed to see the intrinsic value of the whole body of Christ, it has caused wounds to its own body. The wounds and fissures caused by theological differences regarding human sexuality are tragic and ongoing and, frankly, exhausting. Historically, many churches have variously rejected, "welcomed but not affirmed," ignored, and actively harmed LGBTQ people. These actions and attitudes are based on theological decisions made by congregations and denominations. Like pawns in a theological game, queer people have been the subjects of dispute. I want to emphasize that in these debates, LGBTQ people have not been the problem; that is, the debates and arguments have not been caused or exacerbated by the LGBTQ members of the church. Instead, the debates have focused on heterosexual folks debating the theological appropriateness of certain expressions of sexuality, with queer people often caught in the middle. This whole painful process has unfolded differently in different denominations, but it is certainly a conversation that is occurring in all mainline traditions. As we shall see, it has been a time of great harm for the whole church.

This great harm attests to the need for healing. Queer people need justice and straight people need mercy. One of the means of seeking justice and mercy available to us is the pulpit. The Bible, interpreted by love, is a balm for healing. So it can be for the church's relationship to sexuality—preaching can provide structure and faithful content to an ongoing conversation about sexuality within the church. As with all subjects that matter deeply to the life of the church, sexuality must find its way into the pulpit.

Preachers must address this topic because the lives of LGBTQ people literally depend on the proclamation of good news about sexuality. Young people are dying because some churches have been silent on this issue and others have offered nothing but condemnation. People are facing unimaginable suffering and trauma because they have been rejected by people they love. This topic is important because if we are to be fully human we must be able to recognize the image of God imprinted on every human person. We acknowledge that this image has been blurred by human sin, but the equation of sin and sexuality has resulted in great harm to LGBTQ people. It is important that we preach about sexuality because it is a deeply theological and biblical issue that shapes our ethics and our attitudes. It is also important to remember because sexuality should be a source of joy and contentment, and that is what we see modeled in the lives of many queer people.

## Introduction

The LGBTQ community has something to teach the church about authenticity and joy.

In terms of ethics, there is a gospel imperative to participate in the reconciling love of God most fully revealed in Jesus Christ. This involves our own confession and release from guilt and shame. It also involves a movement toward others, to be reconciled not only with our neighbors but also with ourselves and with God. The relationships among the church and LGBTQ communities are broken, and as long as the church fails to honor the lives and witness of people with all sexual identities, it remains fractured.

## DEFINING TERMS AND ASSUMPTIONS

Rather than rehearsing the biblical and theological arguments related to human sexuality, I am beginning with several key assumptions about sexuality. First, sexuality is simply the way that people experience themselves as sexual beings—physically, emotionally, socially, spiritually, etc. Second, sexuality is a good gift from God but is at risk of being marred by sin. In our most intimate relationships, we are vulnerable to causing each other pain. Third, I am assuming that all humans are sexual beings and that there is a range of expressions of sexuality—and I maintain an openness to all these expressions. Fourth, I am assuming that LGBTQ Christians are valuable and irreplaceable members of the body of Christ.

After referencing the term LGBTQ in a sermon, I was asked, "What do all the letters mean?" This was a reminder of the importance of defining the terms used in the pulpit and not assuming that everyone knows what we mean by terms like LGBTQ. The terminology that grounds this project stretches and grows and will mean different things in different communities. There are different opinions about all these terms. Austin Hartke offers two general rules for talking about the LGBTQ community. First, although there is comfort in clear definitions, language is constantly changing and definitions shift. Second, always prioritize the definition of the person standing in front of you.[1] Sexual orientation here is about sexual and romantic attraction. Sexual/gender identity is more psychological and refers to the internal sense of one's gender. Sexual/gender expression "has to do with the way you act out gender through things like clothing, hair, voice and mannerisms."[2] Heterosexual refers to those individuals whose sexual orientation is straight—they are attracted to members of the opposite sex. Cisgender refers to those individuals whose gender and identity matches their sex assigned at birth. When I use the term "heterosexual" I mean cisgender heterosexual. In this book, I use two main terms to refer to sexual and gender minorities—LGBTQ and queer. I will use the acronym LGBTQ to mean lesbian, gay, bisexual, transgender, and queer or questioning. While I have chosen this acronym for its brevity, my intention is also to include those who are asexual, intersex, two-spirited, or anything other than heterosexual.[3] Lesbian refers to women who are attracted to other women, while gay men are attracted to other men. Bisexual refers to those who are attracted to men and women. Transgender people's gender identity does not match the sex they were assigned at birth. All these terms are much richer than I can communicate in this brief description.[4]

"Queer" is a controversial term in some circles, and some will raise their eyebrows that it has been included here. Some people are reluctant to use it because they perceive it to be slur. Some LGBTQ people do not like the term either, for various reasons. However, it is a term that challenges the status quo and upsets the binaries that divide the world. Bridget Rivera writes: "Gay people don't call themselves gay and lesbian because they define themselves by sex. Rather, such language is a response to the sexual stigma of society. As long as LGBTQ people experience dehumanization because of sex and gender, they will need a vocabulary to name that experience and ultimately reclaim their humanity. Queer language

1. Hartke, *Transforming*, 24.
2. Hartke, *Transforming*, 27.
3. A more complete acronym would be LGBTQ2SIA+.
4. See Hartke, "Beginner's Guide to Gender," chapter 2 in *Transforming*.

## INTRODUCTION

therefore challenges how the world would otherwise define the queer experience."[5] I choose to use the term "queer" because I find it to be an inclusive term that allows for a variety of sexual and gender identities and expressions. The terms "LGBTQ" and "queer" represent a very broad set of communities that are likely more different than they are similar.

Another key term for this project is "to affirm." I am building toward an affirming perspective on preaching. The Oxford English Dictionary defines affirm as "to state as a fact; to assert strongly and publicly; to offer emotional support or encouragement."[6] Affirming preaching states loudly and publicly that LGBTQ people are welcome and included in the sacred space, and it offers emotional support and encouragement to those who are struggling with their own sexuality or the sexuality of others. This includes supporting and encouraging those who have a negative view of sexual diversity as they wrestle with their own worldviews and theologies, especially as sexual diversity relates to faith. Affirmation goes beyond raising a rainbow flag, pompoms, and multicolored cakes. It includes an affirmation of faith—that we belong to a God who makes space for all of us. It is an ongoing process of offering hospitality even to those with whom we disagree vehemently. At the same time, it is preaching that prioritizes the safety of those who have been harmed most directly.

### FINDING MY VOICE

The story of Christ's body in the world is a story of pain and exclusion, welcome and acceptance. It is the church's story—a story that will cause shame and discomfort as well as bring joy. For many years, I was afraid to preach about human sexuality and the full inclusion of LGBTQ people in the church. I am a seasoned preacher and teacher of preaching in a denomination that has agonized over human sexuality for a long time. It is perhaps surprising that I did

---

5. Rivera, *Heavy Burdens*, 59.
6. Oxford English Dictionary, s.v. "affirm (v.)."

not broach this topic. I have been hopeful for the full inclusion of LGBTQ individuals in the life of the church for many years. Certainly, LGBTQ examples find their way into my sermons and my prayers as I talk about human celebration and suffering, but for a long time I did not preach any sermon that directly advocated for honoring the sexuality of all people, including LGBTQ people. This is a point of shame and confusion for me. Why would I not preach about such a vitally important topic? There are several reasons why the subject of my preaching has not aligned with my theology and my commitments to the LGBTQ community.

First, it was uncomfortable and awkward to talk about sex. Perhaps others are braver than I, but I found preaching about sexuality to be akin to talking to my parents about the birds and bees. If the preacher is uncomfortable, so are the congregants! Second, knowing that congregations are diverse, with a variety of positions and perceptions, I was afraid of dividing the congregation by preaching affirmation when not all agreed that this was appropriate theology. There was a fear that they wouldn't like me, that they would be angry with me. I dreaded the conversations at the door after church. My beliefs on the matter are so strongly held that I was reluctant to encounter alternative perspectives. I did not feel equipped to defend my position, partly because it makes me feel so emotional. In other words, I was not confident in my ability to preach an effective sermon based on the reactions I might receive from others. This fear has led me to remain silent when I should have been resisting the rhetoric of exclusion which is proclaimed rather loudly. Martin Luther King Jr. once said that silence, when it goes on long enough, is an act of betrayal. My failure to speak has been an act of betrayal to both my baptismal and my ordination vows and an act of betrayal toward the LGBTQ community within the church and beyond. This book is, in part, a response to that failure to speak loudly enough about God's infinite love, mercy, and justice. It is a response strongly rooted in the belief that all are children of God, that all belong.

In conversation with a friend from my teenage days, we reflected on the freedom that young people feel today in naming

# Introduction

their own sexuality. We did not feel that freedom, nor did it even occur to us to want it. Yet, thinking back, how many of my friends would have been helped by a theology that held open possibilities for sexuality. In retrospect, I realize that my understanding of human sexuality was extremely underdeveloped even into my adulthood. Although I advocated for affirmation, I really had not reflected on the true diversity and variety of human beings in terms of their gender and sexuality. My denomination, for example, has been fixated on gay people but has largely ignored the experience of transgender or non-binary people. I have struggled to address people by the correct pronouns, not out of any rejection of their identities but because I've been so conditioned by the culture to think only in terms of "he" and "she." There is a steep learning curve associated with preaching toward affirmation regardless of our own experience of sexuality and gender.

All these factors were complicated by the fact that my perspective did not align with the official position of my denomination. There was a two-decade period in which my denomination stayed largely silent on human sexuality. It is now clear that this silence caused tremendous harm not only to the LGBTQ community but also to the church. We have spent many years denying the full participation of LGBTQ people—rejecting their gifts. So much has been lost along the way, as LGBTQ church leaders have been ignored, marginalized, or denied ordination. All those gifts that might have been used to build up and transform the church were rejected. Amazingly, LGBTQ people have continued to build up and transform the church, often through alternative channels. The generosity of this work is beyond measure, as LGBTQ people have continued to minister even when the church did not honor their gifts.

In truth, I didn't know how to preach in a way that would honor the lives and ministries of people of all sexual identities. No one ever taught me how to preach about sexuality or how to navigate an issue for which there is so much emotion and varying opinion. While I was continually supportive and affirming behind the scenes, I regret that my preaching did not contribute to the movement of the Spirit which was acting to bring about change in the denomination. Others courageously fought this battle.

Gradually and painfully, my denomination is moving toward the affirmation of LGBTQ people. As in most denominations, there is a great deal of work to be done. For example, denominational decisions need to filter down to the congregational level where they can be enacted in the life of the people. That is the context in which this book arises. As my denomination began to make decisions about marriage and ordination, there arose a need to equip congregations to have conversations about sexuality. Some are seeking to become affirming. Others are struggling with conflict. Still others are altogether silent on the matter. What kind of preaching will support generous and loving engagement on the issues surrounding sex and sexuality? This is, in part, the story of my own journey as a person who loves the church and is ashamed of the church simultaneously. As a homiletician, I have insights to share about the theology and practice of preaching. As an ally (I hope!) of the LGBTQ community, I have much to learn. This is my journey of discovery as I learned to put my passion into words and urge the church toward a positive and affirming vision for human sexuality.

I write from the privileged position of a white, Canadian settler, highly educated and resourced, cisgender, straight, married, Presbyterian woman. Even as I write this, I realize how difficult it is for me to identify and name my social location and various identities. Until recently, it never would have occurred to me to include my gender or settler identity in a biographical listing. Preachers whose identities resemble mine may need to learn the art of naming things that were never spoken previously—things like race, gender, and colonial identity. While we often expect LGBTQ persons to identify themselves as such, heterosexuals rarely name their own sexual identity insofar as it has been considered normative. Heteronormativity is "the explicit or implicit and pervasive assumption by individuals and societies that heterosexuality is the norm for biological sex, gender identity, sexual orientation, and sexual relationships."[7] As Askew and Allen remind us, "When we

---

7. Askew and Allen, *Beyond Heterosexism*, 4.

## INTRODUCTION

speak of God's care for society, we should name heterosexism as easily and often as we name discrimination related to race, age, sex, class, religion, and ability."[8]

Those with identities that have been considered normative can learn to recognize the ongoing harm that is being done by heteronormativity. I confess that I have been part of the harm, and in this book I hope to engage in a respectful conversation with LGBTQ theologies in hopes of midwifing a church that is more faithful to Jesus and is equipped to engage in a process of reconciliation. While much of my experience in the Presbyterian Church in Canada (PCC) is reflected here, the material in these pages will be valuable for preachers from any denomination that struggles with debates over human sexuality.

Writing from my particular social location means that there are things I do not understand because I have not lived them. I have wondered about whether it is appropriate for me to write this book as a straight person, yet I strongly believe that those who have been most responsible for the hurt must do the serious work of reclaiming grace. The work of repairing the damage belongs to the whole church—which includes a significant number of LGBTQ persons. However, the onus of responsibility is on those who are not LGBTQ. Just as when we approach issues such as settler-Indigenous relationships or the relationship between white people and people of color, those who have offended must take the lead on repair by confessing, apologizing, naming harm, and making decisions that will reduce future pain. We can do so only as we are in conversation with those who have been harmed. Thus, this book engages LGBTQ perspectives on theology and scriptural interpretation and reflects a variety of ongoing conversations within the church and beyond.

## PREACHING AND SEXUALITY

Some might argue that preaching about sexuality is too political or controversial for Christian worship. This preaching is political,

---

8. Askew and Allen, *Beyond Heterosexism*, 9.

and it is controversial, but it is also necessary for the reasons I have stated above, including the need to preach good news about sexuality to those who have suffered exclusion and hatred. When the body of Christ is broken, the sermon can contribute to healing. If sermons are to contribute to healing, they must be both pastoral and prophetic. Feminist homiletician Christine M. Smith urges us not to make too fine a distinction between pastoral and prophetic. "When we enable people to understand the powers and forces in this world that close family farms, bring genocide into Native American communities nation-wide, lock women into homes of violence, and force gay and lesbian persons to deny the loves in their lives, we are preaching pastorally and prophetically, and we are addressing individual and collective human need."[9] This means treading gently when we know that some in the pews will disagree with us. We must have compassion for those who are caught in systems of heteronormativity.[10] It also means speaking firmly against the powers of hate and discrimination, bringing to light the marvelous love that God has for all creation, including those who are not heterosexual. This kind of preaching is deeply unsettling, as it causes us to examine our own biases, misconceptions, and dangerous theologies. It is also highly constructive insofar as it attempts to build toward more redemptive perspectives and theologies.

Recently, it has become clear to me that preachers need tools to do this work. We simply do not know what to do to adequately address sexuality in our midst. This is perhaps one of the reasons that so many have remained silent—there is no clear pathway toward affirming preaching in a context of debate and division. I hoped to find clear advice about how to do this challenging work of encouraging a congregation toward affirmation. I found companionship in a few places, including Emily Askew and O. Wesley Allen's *Beyond Heterosexism in the Pulpit* and Christine M. Smith's *Preaching as Weeping, Confession and Resistance*.[11] Askew and Al-

---

9. Smith, *Preaching as Weeping*, 163.

10. Askew and Allen, *Beyond Heterosexism*, 6.

11. See Askew and Allen, *Beyond Heterosexism*, and Smith, *Preaching as Weeping*. Askew and Allen facilitate a conversation about preaching that is

## INTRODUCTION

len's book, which will be referenced throughout this volume, offers clear and useful strategies for ridding the pulpit of heterosexism. Smith also offers important insights about heterosexism that contribute meaningfully to preaching that affirms. What I did not find was a book that could help me address preaching and sexuality in a holistic way. Beyond avoiding heterosexism, how might a preacher think through all the pieces of preaching that affirms sexuality?

Olive Hinnant has written a valuable book entitled *God Comes Out: A Queer Homiletic*.[12] Her work is a "transformational, prophetic homiletic for out clergy and straight allies."[13] She highlights the lack of homiletical literature that acknowledges the presence of LGBTQ people in the church's history of preaching.[14] For Hinnant, coming out is a powerful image for homiletics. She constructs a homiletical theory from the perspective of a self-identified lesbian, white minister. She asks, "Is it possible for God to come out through the preaching voices of those whose lives can honestly reflect and reveal the vivid ways God's diversity in human life is lived?"[15] This text is helpful for uplifting and encouraging LGBTQ preachers and celebrating their gifts to the field of homiletics.

Sexuality is a complex topic, and preaching cannot do all the heavy lifting. Our preaching will be more effective if it is accompanied by conversation. Preaching is a conversation—engaging the preacher, the worship participants, the text, the culture, and the Holy Spirit. Preaching, in the context of the liturgy, remains one of the primary ways we are shaped as worshipping communities. It forms our ethics and our attitudes, educates us, and corrects us. I am assuming here that preaching, as a formative practice, has the potential to inspire the church toward new ways of being, thinking, and behaving. While it cannot be our only

---

addressing forms of discrimination about homosexuals or "gays." While much of what they say can be applied to other expressions of human sexuality, the book does not address a broad spectrum of sexualities.

12. Hinnant, *God Comes Out*.
13. Hinnant, *God Comes Out*, 9.
14. Hinnant, *God Comes Out*, 8.
15. Hinnant, *God Comes Out*, 17.

means of communication, it is a highly significant one. However, conversations about human sexuality should extend beyond the sermon—through Bible study, denominational study guides, and participatory seminars.

If you are searching for words to speak about sexuality from the pulpit you will find companionship in these pages. This is not a process or a model but, rather, a posture of remembering.

## REMEMBERING THE BODY

The title of this volume, *Remembering the Body*, is meant to be evocative of three things. The first is that we remember the importance of the body—literal, physical bodies, and the ways that those bodies connect to other bodies. The church has historically undervalued the physical body in favor of the spiritual realm. If we are going to talk about sex, we need to remember that we are talking about flesh and blood. When we "remember" the body we recall the primacy of our physical experience—acknowledging that we interact with the world in parcels of bone and skin. Sex in the most basic sense is the relationship of one body to another. Preaching that affirms will take seriously the demands and needs of the human body—its appetites, its wounds, its pleasures. It remembers that there is a deep connection between sexuality and spirituality.

Second, in the church we are connected to other bodies in a construct that Paul called the body of Christ—an ecclesiological model that describes a way of being the church. The body of Christ is broken, and it needs to be re-membered, reconnected. While it is a gruesome image, the body of Christ has harmed itself by cutting off its members. Perhaps there is still opportunity for healing. It remains to be seen whether the pieces can be stitched back together: and even if they can, the scars will remain. This kind of preaching aims to heal that which has been disconnected, separated, cut off.

Third, this language of remembering draws us back to sacramental remembrance—the memories of water and blood and community. We are invited to remember our baptismal identities—our

## INTRODUCTION

truest, most genuine characters. Preaching calls us back to ourselves, calls us to embrace our deepest and truest identities.

To remember is not to return to some past state. This is not idealized memory, nor does it involve rose-colored glasses. To remember is to "have in or be able to bring to one's mind an awareness of (someone or something that one has seen, known, or experienced in the past)."[16]

To remember is to know again. Perhaps in a sense, to return to ourselves. We have a faith tradition that calls us to remember God's mighty acts. We remember the creation. We remember the exodus. We remember Calvary. We remember the empty tomb. We remember the waters of baptism that flowed over us, and we remember Christ in bread and wine. We remember small acts of mercy. We remember the stories of people of faith that are preserved in the Scriptures, and we remember the theologies of the church that have taken faithful guesses at God's identity. We remember that we are situated within a particular living organism that is the body of Christ. Each part of that body belongs, and each part relates to the whole. Part of this process is coming to terms with our treatment of our own body. We need to remember delight, and nurture, and sabbath—those gifts of care for our bodies.

There is a lot to remember, and a lot that has been forgotten. For example, the body of Christ has a collective amnesia about how to care for each of its parts. It has forgotten how to function as a body, and thus caused harm to its own members. We have also forgotten the absolute pleasure of sex. I have chosen this language of remembering because I believe that part of the process of becoming more affirming is to remember who we are and to whom we belong. Somewhere along the way the church has forgotten Jesus' basic instructions to his disciples. The body of Christ has sometimes forgotten its baptismal promises, and in some cases its ordination vows. What can the body of Christ remember about itself and its Creator that will lead to more robust and inclusive relationships? The following chapters reflect on the constructive theological work of reclaiming the body and affirming the variety

---

16. Oxford English Dictionary, s.v. "remember, (v.1)."

of sexual identities present in the church and beyond. It aims to equip preachers with tools and resources which will support the healing of the broken body of Christ.

Chapter 1 aims to reclaim the body and sex as a positive construct for the pulpit. Rooted in the incarnation of Jesus Christ, preaching should care for human bodies and center bodies in the pulpit. Homophobia/transphobia, heteronormativity, and trauma are stumbling blocks to preaching about sexuality. How might sermons heal these wounds in order to preach a faithful, body-centered gospel that honors human sexuality?

Chapter 2 develops the image of the church as the body of Christ—an incarnate, vulnerable body prone to both intense woundedness and intense joy. In our baptisms we become members of the body of Christ. This chapter outlines some of the damage that has been done to the church as whole by debates about human sexuality. A task of preaching is to teach the body how to care for itself, how to honor all its parts—an ethic of care presumed by the practice of baptism. In its brokenness and collective trauma, the body of Christ has forgotten its baptismal identity. I argue for preaching that remembers a joyful and inclusive baptismal identity that celebrates human sexuality in all its diversity, as well as re-membering the body that has been dismembered by exclusion. A task of preaching is to move the community toward reclaiming baptismal identity.

Chapter 3 builds on the classic work of Christine M. Smith to look at preaching about sexuality as acts of weeping, confession, and resistance. Preaching is a public theological naming of reality in the face of radical evil. We lament and mourn, we tell the truth, and we provide tools for resisting evil. Through an exploration of the Presbyterian Church in Canada's 2022 Confession to God and the LGBTQ community, I consider the types of confession that are needed. Moving beyond homophobic/transphobic, heteronormative theologies, we can preach toward affirmation of all sexualities.

Chapter 4 probes the possibility of reconciliation for a body of Christ that has been divided on the issues surrounding human sexuality. Despite the hurt on all sides, we are members of one

INTRODUCTION

body and belong to each other. In an ethos of conflict, the sanctuary may not be a safe space for everyone. Unity, while remaining a hope, is problematized by the kinds of forced unity that arise in oppressive settings. Forgiveness between human persons remains a possibility, especially as the body is nurtured and connective tissues between persons and groups are strengthened by baptismal identity.

Chapter 5 reflects on the nature of biblical interpretation for preaching sermons that affirm human sexuality. Drawing on queer biblical interpretation, it outlines tools and resources that enable positive preaching about human sexuality and diversity. The Bible has been a source of liberation and oppression. Interpretation is a communal task that links to the larger conversations of a community. Preachers are invited to wonder about the implications of the text for human bodies, for the body of Christ, and for the queer community.

Chapter 6 builds toward a posture of affirmation in preaching. This kind of preaching remembers the body, remembers the body of Christ, and remembers its baptismal identity. By protecting the body, offering hospitality, and rooting the community in baptismal promises, sermons can open a space in which all are received with love and a sense of belonging.

Chapter 7 contains three sermons that illustrate the contours of affirming preaching.

In the words of Christine M. Smith, "As preachers, surely a part of our message of liberating grace is that deliverance from fear ultimately demands that we plunge our lives directly into those things we fear the most."[17] To preach in a way that honors the beauty of human sexuality will take a great deal of courage. There is hatred, uncertainty and indifference, ignorance, and a whole history of avoidance and embarrassment that occupies the pews, and this process is about unsettling some of those emotions. As a preacher, you may feel intimidated, even frightened, by the thought of engaging worship participants on the topic of human sexuality. I rarely get nervous in the pulpit, but preaching these

17. Smith, *Preaching as Weeping*, 107.

kinds of sermons gave me butterflies. It is only because of God's grace that we can hope for change. We belong only to God in Jesus Christ, and our preaching must be faithful to the calling that accompanies our belonging.

# 1

# Preaching and the Body

## EMBODIED BEINGS

> And, ah, the lips of that lovely mouth—
> a ribbon of scarlet.
> Your temples, behind that veil,
> glow like the halves
> of a freshly sliced pomegranate. (Song of Songs 4:3)[1]

SONG OF SONGS IS poetry that celebrates human love in the context of creation. As a teenager I giggled helplessly at the idea that a lover was like a gazelle traipsing over the hills, or that their appearance might be compared to halved fruit. For many of us, the blatant language of love and desire is uncomfortable because we have been raised with a particular distaste for the body, a distaste for the intermingling of spirituality and sexuality. In fact, the intimacy of the language in this biblical text might astonish us—why on earth is such an earthy, almost primal description of human love located right in the middle of the Bible? Someone somewhere thought that this piece of poetry mattered enough to be included in the canon of scripture. I am glad it is there. It reminds us that

1. Priests for Equality, *Inclusive Bible*, 1543.

we were created as embodied beings. Our intellect, our spirituality, our sexuality: all are housed in vulnerable, changing bodies. Our shared life in Christ is also body-shaped. This chapter argues for the centering of the body in theological discourse and pastoral practice, particularly the practice of preaching.

Encased in flesh and surging with hormones, we are sexual beings by nature. Sexuality positions us in relation to one another in intimate ways—it is an essential part of how we connect to others. Some churches are talking about sex too much—it is dominating their courts and their conversations. Others are not talking about it at all—ignoring opportunities to preach gospel news about a topic that concerns us so powerfully. Our sexuality, while complicated, is also God-breathed. It is thus to be celebrated and nurtured from the pulpit. Sex affects us to the core of our beings, so it is no wonder that there are strong feelings and opinions about sexuality, especially sexuality in relation to religion. There is a full spectrum of emotion about sexuality in the church. Christians are ill-prepared to have conversations about sexuality in fruitful ways, judging from the degree of ire raised by the very mention of sexuality.

Our culture is obsessed with sex—what is being taught in schools, what is shown on the internet, the right of individuals to choose what they wear and how they represent themselves—all of this is up for debate. Increasingly, there are attacks on the human rights of those who identify as LGBTQ. Sadly, many of these attacks are perpetrated by Christians. We exist in an unstable time when human rights are in jeopardy and misinformation abounds. It is time for preachers to hone their skills for equipping the church to engage lovingly in conversations about sexuality. By centering the human body in a discourse about sexuality, we are attending to the obvious—that sexuality and bodies are inextricably linked. The church's conversation about sexuality is a conversation about real bodies. These bodies may be safe or in danger. They may be whole or harmed. Our preaching must address the body and sexuality.

The year I started seminary my cohort registered for the history of Christianity course. At the time we were all mystified by the professor's choice of textbook (keeping in mind that this was a general introduction to the history of the church). *The Body and Society: Men, Women and Sexual Renunciation in Early Christianity*[2] seemed an odd choice for a group of Protestant MDiv students, and I don't think we ever received a satisfactory explanation. We just could not imagine what the body had to do with church history. I confess that I did not learn much about sexuality or the history of the church in that course. In retrospect I am inspired by the idea of looking at church history through the lens of sexuality. Scholars and practitioners are learning, gradually, to recognize the impact of sexuality and gender on all facets of life and to interpret Scripture with sexuality and gender in view. History has everything to do with the body. History is, after all, about remembering bodies—what we ate, where we slept and who we slept with, how we arranged our daily lives, who we fought with and why, how we used our bodies for worship and work. As we remember the history of the church, we are not remembering merely spiritual beings but real physical bodies who worked and worshipped in the fullness of their embodied nature. One of the reasons that sexuality has dominated conversations in the church is that bodies matter so much. It may seem obvious that bodies matter—these flesh and blood and bone parcels that are animated with spirit. None of us can function without our body. It cannot be overstated that part of Christian nurture, and the role of preaching, is to honor and protect the physical bodies of people.

How should we begin a conversation about preaching and sexuality? My initial instinct was to begin with God as the Creator and originator of all sexuality. Maybe I should begin with the people who would be listening to these sermons, and whom I would be asking to wrestle with these tough realities. Maybe I should begin with scriptural interpretation. Or church doctrine. Maybe I should begin with baptism, as the source of Christian identity and belonging. Or hospitality. Or with the troubling news about human sin and the ways that Christians have sinned against LGBTQ persons. As I searched my imagination for an order or

2. Brown, *Body and Society*.

direction for approaching this kind of preaching, it was the word "incarnation" that came to me repeatedly. The place where God meets us. The space of "God with Us." I decided to begin at the center of God's revelation, Jesus Christ.

What does it mean to begin with Jesus Christ? Jesus' ministry is incarnational and always relational—concerned about the relationships between people and their relationship with God. Jesus spent a lot of time resisting theologies and worldviews that point away from abundant life, offering instead hope for healing and repair of what is broken. Jesus was concerned about actual bodies—hungry, hurting bodies. He interrogated the hemorrhaging woman because he cared about her body and its healing. He fed the five thousand, which not only showed his prowess at conjuring a meal but also his compassion for a big group of people who were getting hangry. Jesus lived in flesh, suffered the torments of being human, experienced the joys. He died a brutal, violent death and was raised up into a physical body that still bears the wounds of suffering.

> Bodies matter so much that Jesus came back from death in his own body, in that same despised, abused, and tortured body. It's an incredible picture of solidarity, not an embrace of violence. It is a reminder that the exclusion, diminishment, and dehumanization of bodies are still realities in the world and that Jesus Christ, Emmanuel, that is "God-with-Us" means way more than empathy.[3]

Christian theology must take seriously the fact that we live and move and have our being in embodied ways. Jesus' incredible act of solidarity was to wear flesh and blood, to experience the fullness of living in a human body. The body of Christ connects our human bodies to other human bodies through water, bread, and blood. The topic of human sexuality is very obviously about bodies—about the ways we are created to enjoy our bodies and the dangers of abusing them. The potential for trauma and healing resides in the body. In addition, sexuality and spirituality have been divorced from each other when instead they are intertwined.

---

3. Kim-Kort, *Outside the Lines*, 74.

## Preaching and the Body

As you can see, a focus on Jesus Christ led immediately to a focus on the human body. A christological lens will invite us to perceive the well-being of human bodies as central to the task of preaching. What would it mean if we were to center the body in preaching? A local pastor who ministers to a small group of quite elderly people regularly preaches sermons forty to fifty minutes long. In my tradition, this is an exceptionally long sermon. This preacher is not paying attention to the bodily needs of his congregation. For many seniors, it is difficult to sit for an extended period. Many of them must return to their lodgings for lunch at a particular time, and a long sermon throws those plans into disarray. This is a small example of how a sermon can either care for the body or ignore its needs. We are accustomed to modulating our voices so that people can hear us, for example. How often, however, do we think about the physical bodies of those among whom we preach? Listeners are flesh and bone, with aches and pains and growling stomachs. Pain and emptiness will interfere with their ability to hear what you have to say. A young mom is preoccupied with feeling her baby kicking in her womb. An older man is aware of the fullness of his bladder. The choir director is contemplating her recent cancer diagnosis, feeling physically ill at the thought of treatment options. There will be listeners who come bearing the wounds of violent domestic abuse. Teenagers whose brains have not yet finished developing. Seniors who are preoccupied with the availability of a ride home and are unable to focus on message of the sermon. The internal workings of our bodies and the way those bodies move around in the world are of concern to the preacher.

In other words, we are entrusted with a group of bodies for a short time on a regular basis. How do we honor those bodies during the sermon time?

Concern for the bodies of listeners goes beyond caring for their bodies in the actual preaching moment. How does the content of our preaching support and nurture human bodies? Preaching should be concerned with the safety, well-being, and satiety of the community—a community that extends well beyond the local to the entire body of Christ in the world. Our preaching has implications for bodies beyond the church as well, insofar as Christians are tasked with feeding the hungry, visiting the sick and imprisoned, and liberating oppressed bodies.

## CENTERING BODIES IN THE PULPIT

Despite the inescapability of our embodied nature, the church tends to cut off mind from body. As a Presbyterian, I am most comfortable in a worship setting that separates mind from body. The Reformed tradition removed some of the visual and olfactory elements of worship, resulting in an experience of worship that heavily favors the mind over the body.[4] Somewhere along the way the church has lost the language of embodiment. Sexuality has been cut off from spirituality. The problem is that when we do not talk about sex we are hindered in our relationship with God and with others. Kim-Kort perceives that there is room for desire within Christian theology. "As Christians, we've tended to demonize and vilify sex. But desiring God, wholly and fully, not only makes space for but inspires our pleasure. And then loving a desiring God is a fuller picture of a God who also yearns for our happiness, our joy, and yes, even our pleasure. To reiterate the Westminster Shorter Catechism, this is God's glory."[5] In other words, our bodies are for the glory of God. In all our bodily activity, we belong to God and bring glory to God. Through our work, our play, our connection with other people, our sexuality, we are instruments of God's glory.

Kim-Kort writes about the way she was raised in the church to believe that bodies are good but need to be "clothed and closeted."[6] Her reflection resonated with me—in my family of origin the body was not to be exposed in public. For preachers, it is valuable to think through the beliefs about the body with which we were raised. Are bodies good or bad or neutral? Are bodies to be seen or hidden? To what extent is the body a source of shame

---

4. See Rivera, *Heavy Burdens*, for a fascinating discussion of how the Reformation led to sexual reform within the culture.

5. Kim-Kort, *Outside the Lines*, 16.

6. Kim-Kort, *Outside the Lines*, 69.

or celebration? When you were growing up, was God affirming of your body or judgemental? Thinking back on your experience of church over the course of your lifetime, what messages have you received about the relative value of your body? The answers to these questions will depend primarily on your context—your geography, ethnicity, theological formation, sexual identity. If you are heterosexual, you likely had a different experience than someone who is queer. How do we go about reintegrating mind and body? Kim-Kort argues that a queer perspective is helpful for undoing the mind-body binary.

> From the get-go, queerness undoes this dichotomy between mind and body, and the subsequent marginalization of bodies, by deliberately, purposefully centering bodies: how they move, how they breathe, how they express themselves, and how they experience pain and violence, lust and sex, desire, and intimacy. More than that, queerness recognizes the temptation toward dichotomy and bridges these binaries, healing the gulf. It fills in the spaces we tend to leave empty and makes whole what is broken. A queer spirituality then invites us to see the possibility that our bodies are the sacramental—the holy, ordinary, sacred, and real-world—means in which we receive grace and salvation.[7]

We receive God's gifts as embodied human beings created to rest, eat, play, worship, work, and have sex. The enjoyment of these gifts is sacred—what we touch and handle is sacred. The gifts of God's creation are meant to be enjoyed and celebrated and this includes human sexuality. "Sex is an expression of faith," claims theologian David Jensen.[8] "At the heart of the Christian faith is a wondrous claim that word becomes flesh and dwells among us. This divine embrace of human flesh entails the blessing of sexual life: not as something to escape in order to attain salvation, but to nurture as we grow in faith."[9] Kim-Kort also comments on sal-

---

7. Kim-Kort, *Outside the Lines*, 69–70.
8. Jensen, *God, Desire and a Theology of Human Sexuality*, ix.
9. Jensen, *God, Desire and a Theology of Human Sexuality*, ix.

vation as a "this-moment" experience—we are connected to God through our bodies.

> A queer spirituality entreats us to see that salvation has to do with our bodies, and that salvation isn't about a golden ticket to heaven but about the here and now— our experience in and through our materiality in this moment. Every moment becomes sacramental (holy, set apart, and a space for the Holy Spirit to play), and what seems quotidian becomes a supplication for what is divinely felt: a taste, a sip, a sprinkle of that profound connection.[10]

There is a tendency in theology to focus on eschatology—on God's future, when all will be well, and all manner of things will be well. However, this focus on the future may underestimate the significance of bodies in the here and now. We don't *have* bodies; we *are* bodies! We are bodies that get hungry and lonely, tired, and uncomfortable. Preaching about sexuality will always maintain a connection to the here and now—to material reality. It is deeply concerned with the political—that is, the well-being of the community. Heaven, as essential as it is to our Christian hope, is for later. The body is for now.

> The word politics derives from the Greek word polis, which means "city" or "body of citizens" and therefore has to do with the ways humans live in community. The biblical story is the story of a God who from the very beginning is focused on the world and pays attention to the ways humans live in community, who cares about what we do and how we do it, who desires that we live in love, mutuality, and reverence for creation and for the dignity of all human life.[11]

The way we preach about human sexuality is dependent on the conversations that are already happening within a community of faith. The first time I preached about human sexuality was an unmitigated disaster. I was angry about my denomination's

---

10. Kim-Kort, *Outside the Lines*, 81–82.
11. Gaines-Cirelli, *Sacred Resistance*, loc. 159.

response to the sexuality debates, and I was determined that my congregation was going to share my pain. So, I loaded up a whole sermon with deep confession about the church's actions against LGBTQ people. I pushed and pulled and tried my best to get everyone into the same boat I was sailing. I ignored the context. I ignored the state of the conversation among those people on this topic. I did not care about those who would disagree with me—I made no attempt to bring them along with me or make space for them. The congregation was bewildered. I was so anxious to say the right thing and I ended up saying all the wrong things. I did not contribute to a conversation, I bulldozed my way through the conversation, leaving no room for anyone else. I miscalculated the relevance of my words in that space.

My experience is a cautionary tale that suggests we should engage the topic in a way that honors the conversations that have already been happening within the community. As we interpret the gospel as preachers, we have an opportunity to invite rather than demand accompaniment on the journey toward healing. Building trust with congregations is essential to preaching that affirms sexuality. This failed preaching moment also points to my own wounds. I have been wounded in the discourse about sexuality, even though I am not LGBTQ. Those wounds affect the way I approach and construct sermons. In my case, this traumatic wounding prevents me from speaking easily about sexuality, especially sexual identity. I have witnessed brutal and violent conversation even in the courts of the church. I am afraid that I will encounter vitriol. In the sermon I described above, I was defensive—the "hit them with a big stick" mode of homiletic practice. What I needed to do was pay attention to my own wounds. What wounds are carved into my body because of my own painful experiences? How do those wounds shape me as a preacher?

If we are going to center the body in the task of preaching, it is necessary to think about the body of the preacher. We enter the pulpit as physical beings using physical means to impart a particular gospel message. We enter the pulpit as sexual beings with a particular perspective on life and faith that is determined in some way by our sexuality. Our sexuality does not define us entirely, of course, but it is a significant aspect of personhood. It should "show up" in the pulpit—our queerness or straightness. In what ways does the sexuality of the preacher shape their preaching? Preachers are bodies too. David Taylor writes:

> There is, in fact, nothing neutral whatsoever about the bodies that we bring to worship. We bring bodies that fear failure, rejection, or being out of control. We bring bodies that are burdened by sickness and self-hatred. We bring disfigured and dispirited bodies. We bring bodies that have been scarred by touch and bodies that have been starved of touch. And on account of the insidious effects of sin, we bring broken ways of relating to our own bodies and to the bodies of others who gather with us in a common space of worship.[12]

Lutheran liturgy professor Frank Senn reminds us of the importance of the body in liturgy and particularly the embodied leadership of the pastors, who

> need to be more mindful of the use of their bodies in their leadership roles in the liturgy. Physically present before the assembly or congregation, they move from one location to another in the worship space. They use gestures and postures. They read Scripture, preach sermons, offer prayers and administer sacraments. Sometimes they change or lead singing; sometimes they touch people with the laying on of hands. Worship leaders are constantly using their bodies in a public and visible way. As such, they need to be comfortable with their bodily practice.[13]

Olive Hinnant notes that as preachers, especially for out preachers, acceptance of self is the hardest thing that one will accomplish in life. How we feel about ourselves and our own sexuality will affect how we interpret biblical texts and theological traditions. Writing about the experience of queer preachers, she says "that we accept ourselves and believe that God does also

---

12. Taylor, *Body of Praise*, 18.
13. Senn, *Embodied Liturgy*, ix.

speaks volumes about the wideness of God's mercy. We, who have been the latest despised group in the church, are now in pulpits across America speaking a bold word even before we open our mouths."[14] The very presence of sexual diversity in our midst is a bold statement about God's expansive love. Rather than being a problem or an issue, queer Christians are beloved members of the body of Christ.

## STUMBLING BLOCKS TO PREACHING ABOUT SEXUALITY

If you have ever overseen a tween or teenager, you have faced the challenge of navigating sexuality, which often involves the dreaded "talk." There is no guidebook for this conversation. For generations, parents have been trying to convey moral and practical knowledge about sex to their offspring, mostly without tools and skills. Parents generally rely on their own experience to prepare their children for the birds and the bees. Preachers also don't have a guidebook for talking about sex. Many will lack the confidence and skills to approach the topic in sermons. The topic of sexuality gets avoided altogether because the preacher just doesn't know what to say or how to approach the topic in a sensitive way. Like an unprepared parent, we find ourselves relying only our own personal experience, which is always incomplete. There will be no guidebook that tells us how to approach sexuality from the pulpit in a particular time and place.

The lack of a clear guide is one of the barriers to preaching that affirms sexuality. I have already named some of the reasons why I have found this kind of preaching to be challenging. It is uncomfortable because of the various theological expressions of human sexuality that are present in the church. It is uncomfortable because no one wants to talk about sex from the pulpit! It is uncomfortable because we are in so many ways underprepared to use theological or biblical language to talk about human sexuality

---

14. Hinnant, *God Comes Out*, 7.

in a positive way. You will have your own reasons for finding it challenging to preach affirming sermons, and these reasons will differ dependent on your context and the attitudes of your congregation. Beyond discomfort, we can expect to encounter a variety of responses to this kind of preaching. These responses sometimes form barriers that prevent listeners from hearing what we are trying to say. Despite the centrality of the body in human experience, the church has faltered in its self-talk about sex and sexuality. What prevents us from articulating robust theologies of the body that honor sexuality and sexual identity? Our own woundedness and sinfulness will interfere with our ability to preach life-giving sermons. There are several stumbling blocks that stand in the way of preaching that affirms.

Heterosexism assumes that relationships between men and women are normative and ethically and morally superior to same-sex relationships. "This relational structuring of our social, political and religious life is so foundational that primary relations between people of the same gender are deemed immature at best, and immoral, unnatural and sinful at worst."[15] Like sexism and racism, heterosexism is a form of supremacy and (male) domination.[16] As the dominant culture, heterosexuals have privilege in society. "A part of the world of preachers responding to the injustice of heterosexism and homophobia involves inviting heterosexual persons honestly to discern and take responsibility for their privilege while seeking to critique the ideology and social fabric that produce such inequality."[17] This is a task that takes constant vigilance and careful listening to the experiences of sexual minorities. Homophobia is fear or disgust directed at queer people. The term does not explicitly include trans people, so I will generally use homophobia/transphobia in this book. I am concerned here with two different ways of thinking about homophobia and transphobia. One is systemic, the other is more personal, and I believe that preaching should address both. Homophobia/transphobia can be

---

15. Smith, *Preaching as Weeping*, 94.
16. Smith, *Preaching as Weeping*, 96.
17. Smith, *Preaching as Weeping*, 98.

understood as a systemic oppression that manifests at the local or individual level, as well as the institutional level.[18] Preaching can address both individual attitudes and communally held beliefs. Homophobia and transphobia in individuals and communities can be subtle and even unintentional. Some might even say that the problem is not the fear of LGBTQ folks, but rather heteronormative privilege that governs our thinking and behavior. We are all caught in a system that is heteronormative and patriarchal, and tend to make arbitrary divisions based on sexuality, race, or gender. These divisions have led to violence and rejection for LGBTQ people. We tend to be anxious to distance ourselves from those who are different. It is not difficult to imagine how this kind of fragility might find its way into the process of preaching about human sexuality. The mere suggestion that LGBTQ people should have equal rights and be fully affirmed, included, and celebrated may raise the hackles of some who are insecure about their own sexuality or intimate relationships.

## TRAUMA AND GRIEF

Many disciplines, including homiletics, are addressing the reality of trauma and its impact on our physical, emotional, and spiritual well-being. Perhaps the simplest definition is that trauma is a wound—it is an injury on the soul.[19] Trauma is a response to an event or a series of events in which the pain of the past continues into the present. In no way limited to natural or human disasters, trauma is insidious and affects most of us in profound ways. We can be traumatized, for example, by what we witness happening to someone else, not necessarily something that has happened to us personally. I do not wish to untangle the difference between grief and trauma: both are conditions of human nature that are

---

18. Homophobia/transphobia may also be internalized as shame and disgust about one's own sexual identity. See Fensham, *Misguided Love*, chapter 3.

19. Homiletician Joni Sancken refers to these as soul wounds. See Sancken, *Words That Heal*, and Travis, *Unspeakable*, for comprehensive treatments of trauma and its relation to preaching.

different but related. Both interfere with our ability to talk about sexuality from the pulpit. Human beings differ from one another in their adaptivity and response to trauma. For some, trauma will be debilitating. It will make it difficult to define our own identities and to imagine a future that is free from harm.

My denomination is slowly becoming inclusive of all sexualities. It has taken a long time and a lot of energy to get to this place. Among my queer and non-queer colleagues who fought so hard for inclusion and affirmation, there is a sense of exhaustion. I am noticing that many who have been leaders are dropping back, ready to pass the baton. What I perceive is a valley of dry bones with bodies strewn about—too tired to rise and in some cases too wounded. It is difficult to overestimate the trauma of the process of becoming affirming. A queer friend challenged me to consider the ways that I personally experienced traumatic wounding over the past decades, even as a person carrying straight privilege. As a straight person amid these debates, I have suffered from weariness, bitterness, fear, disappointment, and confusion. Weariness occurs because the battle is long and arduous. Bitterness arises out of the vitriol and poor treatment of LGBTQ friends and colleagues. I have been afraid that my colleagues would miss out on significant ministry opportunities or perhaps leave the denomination altogether. I have been disappointed by the behavior and attitudes of certain colleagues and by the slowness of my denomination to address this important issue in a productive and live-giving way. I have been genuinely confused by the arguments against the inclusion of LGBTQ communities in the church because they contrast so sharply with my own perspectives on the gospel. Together these experiences result in a kind of trauma—a wound on my soul.

LGBTQ members who have been denied the full expression of their sexuality and call to ministry have been wounded. Families within the congregation have experienced deep grief because of the sexuality of family members and the ways sexuality has been dealt with within the family system. Some feel they must choose between their church and their child. There is trauma for queer folks who have been taught their sexual expression, identity, or orientation are sinful, that any deviation from heteronormativity places their very salvation in danger. Imagine the fear this could cause for an individual who places great faith in the church's teaching.

Although I tend not to move in non-affirming circles, I imagine there is trauma there too. Relationships have been strained and broken. Things have been said that cannot be unsaid. There is hurt and harm for everyone involved in conversations about human sexuality. It has been traumatic for queer people to have their identity and value as human beings questioned by well-meaning folks who are genuinely concerned for their salvation. It has been traumatic for congregations who find themselves unable to agree on a path forward. Those who use hateful and oppositional language against queer people may indeed suffer from moral injury—the pain of causing pain to others, even when one perceives that they are in the right.

There is grief because the shape of the worshipping body has changed over time. Old friends are missing from the gathering. Some of them are absent because they have been hurt; others simply refuse to participate in an exclusive organization. In fact, we might find ourselves preaching to a remnant—those who have chosen to remain despite the wounding conversations that have occurred. Division is often felt most keenly in the way it promotes absence. Rather than engage in difficult relationships, people find it easier to leave the church altogether. For those who leave and those left behind, there will be grief.[20]

In my experience, churches are traumatized by their decreasing memberships. As churches are increasingly marginalized and moved from the center of culture, congregations feel the pinch in their budgets and their hearts. They remember a time when the church was full. The church growth industry imagines that it is possible to replenish the pews. It may be, however, that the church's lack of inclusion of LGBTQ people is one of

---

20. For an excellent resource from Wes Allen and Alyce McKenzie, see "Preaching to the Left Behind." They deal with the divisions in the United Methodist Church regarding human sexuality and offer several homiletical strategies for preaching amid division.

the reasons for the steep decline in membership and attendance. Young people are disgusted with a church that they perceive to be homophobic/transphobic. Rivera notes that upwards of 90 percent of non-Christians in the United States perceive the church to be homophobic.[21] We are doing ourselves no favors by excluding anyone. I suspect this is a good part of the reason why mainline denominations are shrinking. We have alienated a significant portion of the population—the queer community and its allies. This trauma of decline may indeed be intermingled with the trauma of exclusion. The church has been injured not only because it has lost out on the ministry of queer people but also because its reputation has been damaged. I was disturbed by a very anti-Christian post by a sexual abuse survivor on the social media platform X. This person levelled a fair but uncomfortable observation—viewing the term "Christian" as a derogatory term and synonymous with homophobia and associated with hatred and misuse of power. There are moments when it is difficult to defend the church's record on caring for human beings, or the planet for that matter. The treatment of LGBTQ folks by the Christian church right up to and including the present day has been dreadful. It is no wonder that many LGBTQ Christians and allies choose not to associate with churches.

Rapidly shifting cultural realities can leave us feeling unmoored. When I was in high school, I was aware of only two genders. Now I am aware that there are dozens. This is a rapid shift that creates a need for greater understanding. At the same time, some may experience grief because their world is no longer familiar. Some will long for a time when sexuality was simpler, and others would just rather not have any conversation about the changes that have occurred in our social understandings of sexuality. I perceive this to be the kind of grief that comes with great change. It will be hard to let go of long-held beliefs and assumptions, especially on foundational issues such as sexuality. Homophobia/transphobia, griefs, and traumas can interfere with our ability to preach well and to listen well. I will return to the subject of traumatic wounding in

---

21. Rivera, *Heavy Burdens*, 16. See also Kinnaman and Lyons, *Unchristian*.

chapter 2, which outlines the damage done to the church through sexuality debates.

## HEALING WOUNDS

Traumatic wounding will manifest in various ways throughout the preaching process. Wounds affect the way that people hear and respond to sermons, and thus the way that preachers approach the craft of preparing sermons in that place. Self-awareness of the preacher, careful listening to the context, and trauma-informed approaches to sermon will aid the preacher in responding to the pain that is present. Future chapters will outline tools for responding to harmful attitudes about sexuality.

As noted above, preaching faithfully and effectively about sexuality requires a certain level of self-knowledge and self-awareness on the part of the preacher. What is your theology of sexuality? What is your social location—how do you define your own identity? How do you relate to those with different opinions and theologies? It is important to know one's own triggers, emotional responses, and fragilities.

It almost goes without saying, but exegesis of the local context is crucial for preaching that affirms. This is a process of being aware of the nature of the ongoing conversations occurring within the congregation about sexuality. What are the attitudes? What is the local theology around sexuality? What are the struggles and conflicts? Listening in to these congregational conversations will support the preacher in understanding the ethos within the congregation around sexuality. These conversations might overlap with conversations occurring at the denominational level.

Trauma-informed approaches to preaching will support the development of sermons that can address some of the trauma present in the sanctuary.[22] For example, trauma-informed sermons may include trigger warnings that help listeners prepare for difficult subjects. One of the hallmarks of trauma informed-theology

---

22. See Sancken, *Words That Heal*, and Travis, *Unspeakable*.

is the primacy of bodily experience.[23] As I have tried to show in this chapter, the physical experience of the body is a vital site of theological inquiry. The human body, while vulnerable, is also a beautiful creation that is to be enjoyed and nurtured. In the next chapter we turn to the body of Christ as an image for divine community. As we examine the body of Christ, seeking a whole healthy body, we discover that the collective body has been wounded by conversations about sexuality. How shall we respond to a wounded body, and how will we heal what is broken?

Preaching that affirms human sexuality is based on a theological affirmation that creation is good, that sex is good, that the body is good. This is not to say that everything we do with our bodies is good, or that all sexual activity is good. We are vulnerable creatures, wounded by our own sinfulness and mistakes as well as those harms we inflict on each other. There are limits to what is good for us. Creation is groaning in labor pains because of the consequences of our errors in relation to one another and the earth. Our bodies, our sexualities are all enmeshed in the messiness that we call human community. As we shall see, the body of Christ fosters a particular ethical stance toward the behavior of a community, especially interpersonal relationships.

---

23. Baldwin, *Trauma-Sensitive Theology*, chapter 1.

# 2

# The Body of Christ

## COMING TO TERMS WITH CHRIST'S BODY

A POSITIVE VISION OF the human body is central to preaching that affirms sexuality. Theologian David Taylor borrows the language of Irenaeus to describe the body's glory in the context of worship: "It is a body that is fully alive in the Spirit-ed company of other bodies who have gathered to worship God as Christ's own body."[1] Each body, together, forms the body of Christ. In Christian worship, our bodies come together as the body of Christ—alive and radiant in the Holy Spirit. Outside of worship, we continue to function in this strange configuration of many bodies made into one body.

The New Testament offers many ecclesiological images that help us to imagine the shape of the Christian community. This chapter suggests some of the characteristics of the body of Christ—incarnate, vulnerable, dynamic, and diverse. The body of Christ has been wounded by debates about human sexuality and homophobic theologies—not only LGBTQ persons but also the whole of the body of Christ has experienced hurt. What wounds are evident in the body and what are the implications of those wounds for the

---

1. Cited in Taylor, *Body of Praise*.

well-being of the body? This chapter argues that there is an ethic of care embedded in our baptismal identity.

In 1 Corinthians, Paul writes:

> The body is one, even though it has many parts; all the parts—many though they are—comprise a single body. And so it is with Christ. It was by one Spirit that all of us, whether we are Jews or Greeks, slaves, or citizens, were baptized into one body. All of us have been given to drink of the one Spirit. And that Body is not one part; it is many. (1 Cor 12:12–14)[2]

It does not seem to be a stretch to include "straight or queer" in Paul's list of those who are baptized into one body. In Romans, we are reminded that each body part has a special function, and that there is an interdependency of the bodies that relate to the one body. "Just as each of us has one body with many members—and these members don't have the same function—so all of us, in union with Christ, form one body. And as members of that one body, we belong to each other" (Rom 12:4–5).[3]

Today, the body of Christ is large and diverse—so diverse that it is impossible to capture the variety present within the body globally. Christians come in every shape and size, every nationality, every sexuality. The diversity of the body of Christ is a thing of great beauty and great challenge. It is impossible to overstate the diversity within the body—in terms of nationality, ethnicity, economic status, colonial status, denomination, sexuality, and gender.

In preaching we address a local body that is intimately connected to the larger body in the world. Of course, our preaching does not solely address the body of Christ; it is overheard by others. Primarily, however, the preaching that happens in the context of a worship service is intended for the body of Christ.

What are the characteristics of the body in the place where you preach? Most of us are familiar with the demographics of our congregations—we come to know people amid their everyday lives as well as during those sacred moments of life and death.

---

2. Priests for Equality, *Inclusive Bible*, 2437.
3. Priests for Equality, *Inclusive Bible*, 2417.

## The Body of Christ

Many of us have been trained to think about diversity within the demographics of our congregations in terms of culture, age, theology—but what about sex and sexuality? We may or may not know about the sexualities of our congregants. There are secrets, and there are simply things we don't know because we don't need to know. However, it is likely useful to assume that there are a variety of sexualities within the congregation and in its larger networks.

In our baptisms, we become members of the body of Christ. We bear Christ's DNA in our own bodies, and together as a church we form a viable structure that mirrors the magnificence of the human body. It is not wise to push a metaphor too far: there are ways that the church is like a human body, and ways that the church is not. This image, however, leaves plenty of room for exploring the nature of the church. I would like to propose that the body of Christ as the church is vulnerable to illness and injury in a similar way to the human body. It is incarnate, insofar as its mission is lived out through the actual bodies of its members. It is dynamic, insofar as it can be healed and transformed. It is diverse—the body of Christ contains multitudes. The church as the incarnate, vulnerable, dynamic body of Christ in the world is prone to intense joy and intense sorrow as its members are healed and harmed.

The body of Christ is incarnate because it is composed of flesh and blood. It is vulnerable to sin, division, forgetfulness. It feels pain, and if one part is hurting this causes pain for all the parts. The term "body of Christ" does not seem to originate with the people of Israel, but rather with the sacramental language used by Paul to describe the eucharistic feast. "This is my Body, Broken for you."[4] Here we again encounter bodily trauma—the brokenness of the body. Christ's body was broken in a violent and evil way, and so we are reminded of the vulnerability of the body of Christ.

We sometimes behave as though the church is inviolable, somehow closer to divine nature than human. I would argue that the body of Christ is more aligned with the experience of vulnerable humanity than it is with divine experience—that is, the body

---

4. 1 Cor 11:24.

of Christ has a human body. It is incarnate and subject to sin and traumatic wounding. In the context of conversations about sexuality, the body of Christ has been wounded and dismembered by exclusion and hate.

The body of Christ is suffering from collective trauma. Homiletician Joni Sancken sees collective trauma as a "wound that we share."[5] Despite the shared experience of wounding, trauma can serve to dissolve the "we" in community as it harms or erodes our sense of connection.[6] In practical terms, this trauma forms a barrier to preaching about human sexuality. It damages our "we-ness."

The debates and the various ways that theological positions have been expressed have damaged the collective body, and the body bears signs of collective trauma. LGBTQ persons, anti-LGBTQ persons, those who don't know what they believe or where they stand, allies—all of them have been harmed. Even those who have been most vitriolic bear the trauma of being perpetrators of spiritual violence, and there is potentially moral injury involved when pastors have contributed to the marginalization of members of their own communities.

The consequences of trauma include reduced ability to hope or make meaning out of a situation. It may be difficult for the traumatized to piece together a coherent narrative, making it difficult for those harmed to tell their own story in their own words. The church has trouble telling its own story when it comes to sexuality because it is so mired in shame and guilt. Memory works in strange ways—we remember what we should forget, and we forget what we should remember. When we are traumatized, the possibility of healing feels as though it is shut down. It may be impossible to imagine a situation in which the body could be whole and functioning again. Traumatized persons lose their sense of agency, failing to believe that their actions can have a positive outcome on a situation. Churches can be immobilized by a lack of agency, not believing that they can solve the conundrum of how to live together amid diversity.

---

5. Sancken, *All Our Griefs to Bear*, 25.
6. Sancken, *All Our Griefs to Bear*, 33.

## The Body of Christ

The body of Christ is not fixed or solid—it is a fluid and dynamic reality that shifts and changes. While we might think of baptism as a very individual experience, the entry of a new body into the whole results in a lot of shifting and changing. We must make room for one another. For me, one of the most intriguing aspects of queerness is the way that identity is not fixed. Identity changes and shifts: "How we understand ourselves is constantly shifting, and it's that slippage that compels me. It's in that slippage where queerness emerges as a means to embrace the gray areas and the ambiguities. In this thin place, the miracle of strange but meaningful life emerges in spite of our lack of preparedness, and it changes us."[7]

By some divine alchemy, the individual parts are formed into one body. This collective is dependent on the healthy functioning of all its parts. As noted above, the body of Christ is vulnerable. While we retain a vision of radiant body, unified and healthy, we understand that the body of Christ today is suffering. Some parts have wounded other parts. Some parts have been cut off—removed from the body altogether—and so the body as a whole suffers. The metaphor is clear. In your own body, if you have pain in one place, you will not be able to function properly. The body of Christ feels the absence of its missing parts keenly, like phantom limbs. The body of Christ does not always recognize its own lack of wholeness. Some of us remain oblivious to the damage that has been done to other parts of the body. This is obviously self-destructive. If we are to ignore pain in one part of the body, the entire being will suffer.

## A WOUNDED COMMUNITY

The body of Christ has been wounded by homophobic/transphobic theologies and heteronormative paradigms that have dismembered the body. For generations, LGBTQ people have been

---

7. Kim-Kort, *Outside the Lines*, 28. While the dominant gender narrative of the Christian church has been heterosexism, queer theologies offer fruitful directions for queering the body of Christ.

the subjects of debate and theological inquiry. Many have been excluded from ministry and even from participation in the life of a congregation. These realities are tragic, ongoing, and point to a need for healing. The damage, however, goes much deeper. "Christian teaching that does not affirm the humanity and the wholeness of sexual and gender minority people does harm. It is not simply a theological debate with different perspectives. It is not simply a matter of gracious disagreement. It is a matter of causing material harm to the point of death."[8] Rivera argues that these debates are like a storm that prevent the gospel from being heard.

> In wide swaths of the church, there's a storm system blocking out the gospel. The pain and trauma experienced by LGBTQ people wouldn't be possible otherwise. That storm system looks like a theological milieu in which all the preceding burdens churn and swirl in different churches and denominations, creating the context in which LGBTQ people simply cannot access life-giving Christianity.[9]

These theological storms are preventing the gospel from being heard, and thus depriving some of Christ's living water.

I began this book with a claim that the body of Christ is broken. Bridget Rivera outlines seven ways that LGBTQ Christians have been damaged by the church.[10] While the church should be a place where we lay our burdens down and gain refreshment together, queer people have carried burdens that are far too heavy—burdens that have been manufactured and shared by other Christians. "Indeed, discrimination against LGBTQ people exists at virtually every level of church involvement, from how sexual and gender minorities experience evangelism, to how they experience discipleship, community, accountability, ministry opportunities, counseling, mentorship, family, and friendship."[11]

---

8. Fensham, *Misguided Love*, 5.
9. Rivera, *Heavy Burdens*, 192.
10. Rivera, *Heavy Burdens*.
11. Rivera, *Heavy Burdens*, 15.

## The Body of Christ

The hurt manifests in diverse ways. Some queer people have perceived that they are forced into celibacy by a theology that claims that sex outside of traditional marriage is sinful. These individuals report being seen as sinners whether or not they live celibate lives. There is spiritual damage from theologies that claim damnation for queer people. "Fearing an eternal damnation from which not even Jesus can save you is a psychological and spiritual terror that no words can fully describe. It cuts LGBTQ people off from the gospel and introduces them to a nightmare religion, a faith in which everything about your eternal destination hinges on sex and gender."[12]

Gay theologian Charles Fensham writes poignantly of the heavy burden of carrying the experience of spiritual abuse. Even in churches where he felt welcomed and loved, there was a dark cloud of shame that "the God I love and embrace, God, whom I believe is a loving and gracious God, would suddenly seem remote, stern, and angry."[13] For Fensham, merely being in a place of worship could trigger these responses.

Some LGBTQ Christians feel they have been abandoned by God. As Rivera writes: "Countless LGBTQ people grow up in churches believing that God hates them—the climax to a story that we've told ourselves about sex and gender that elevates cisgender heterosexuality as the only valid human experience and that labels all other experiences sinful."[14] Just by being queer, some individuals have been accused of breaking the bonds of relationships.

> One of the greatest fears that was articulated again and again was that to be honest and open about one's own identity would break the bonds of community and friendship. That pain would be too much to bear. This has led to a sense of alienation and invisibility for many who identify as LGBTQI and has sometimes led to self-destructive behaviors including substance abuse,

---

12. Rivera, *Heavy Burdens*, 164.
13. Fensham, *Misguided Love*, 14.
14. Rivera, *Heavy Burdens*, 17.

self-harm and even to contemplating or actually taking one's own life.[15]

Many LGBTQ people have found it impossible to be themselves in the church—they have been welcomed and accepted only if they conformed to a heterosexual, cisgender norm. This can lead to the suppression of LGBTQ identity—sometimes pretending to be someone they were not, robbing them of the opportunity to be genuine and authentically themselves.

I mentioned earlier my own lack of vocal advocacy for the queer community. I was silent for a long time, at least from the pulpit. I do not think that I understood what was at stake in staying silent. I am not sure that most preachers today understand the stakes of staying silent on sexuality and inclusion. When I speak of harm being done, I am not talking about mere hurt feelings—I am talking about the profound losses. There are the losses experienced by LGBTQ people within the Christian community. There are losses for the entire body of Christ when affirmation is lacking or lukewarm—we, the body of Christ, are literally contributing to our own woundedness. These wounds are significant and silent preachers contribute to greater harm. If preachers stand by silently while harm happens, they risk becoming part of the problem by abdicating their responsibility to monitor and respond to the health of the body.

Why has this pain been allowed to continue? It has been no secret that individuals and communities have been suffering from exclusionary practices, discrimination, and spiritual violence for generations. The church has allowed it to continue. In fact, some of the loudest voices against inclusion come from within the church. It is incumbent on those who strongly feel the need for justice to speak as loudly as those who speak against it.

Exclusionary practices affect me personally, even though I have never been excluded because of my sexuality. The church's tendency to exclude some people calls into question the integrity of the whole system. My trust falters—if the church excludes

---

15. PCC, Final Report of the Rainbow Communion, 12.

## The Body of Christ

LGBTQ people, might it also exclude me for another reason? Are any of us safe within a community that honors some of its members and rejects others?

Transgender theologian Austin Hartke writes:

> Christianity has been dominated by the voices of those who speak out against the existence, the well-being, and the humanity of transgender people. These voices have sunk into the fabric of American culture, and the result has been a rash of murders that cause no religious outrage, no demand for justice from those who should have cared for the wounded ones on the side of the road. We have closed our ears to the cries of the parents who have lost their children because of toxic theology; we have turned away from the tears of the youth who ask if Jesus can love them just as they are. Too many of those questioning their gender identity have been made to feel that they must choose between God and an authentic and happy life. Not all of the people forced into that decision make it out alive.[16]

If we are to continue to reflect on the image of the body of Christ, it will become apparent that we are talking about a body that harms itself by its own choices. I am afraid that my current imaginings about the body of Christ are gruesome. The body is desperately wounded, bleeding, struggling to breathe. The body has a black eye, a broken arm, and several teeth missing. Its choice to hate some of its own parts has backfired, and what was cut off has become an abscessed mess. This is a body that has forgotten how to care for itself. It has forgotten the value of all its parts and ignored the wounds. "This open wound in the Body of Christ continues to impact us all and must be addressed urgently and as the work of the Spirit."[17] How does the body of Christ learn self-love and acceptance? What does care look like within the body? The metaphor is imperfect, yet it presents us with an ethic of care.

---

16. Hartke, *Transforming*, 20.
17. PCC, Final Report of the Rainbow Communion, 5.

# Remembering the Body

## PREACHING AND THE CARE OF THE BODY

Sermons teach the body of Christ how to care for itself. Paul talks about the parts that have less honor—aren't those the parts that require special attention and care? How do we pay attention to our wounded parts? I realize that this begins to sound like an exercise in group psychology. My therapist is always asking me to pay attention to my wounded parts. But as a Christian community, how do we tend to the parts of the community that are suffering? I perceive that preaching tends wounds in at least three ways: preaching points to the wounds and names them; it offers a healing balm—rooted in Scripture and experience; and it proclaims a new possibility for connection and relationship.

One of the consequences of the COVID-19 pandemic was that we became more aware of our own bodies in public spaces. We were keenly aware of how close we were standing to other people in the early days of social distancing. In churches, we spread ourselves around the sanctuary so that we were safely apart. It was an odd experience to automatically reach out to shake someone's hand and then realize that touching is not allowed. We were aware of not coughing in public and the value of sneezing into our elbows. Washing our hands became an art form as we sought to expel every germ. Self-monitoring for every sniffle was everyone's responsibility. We were hyper-aware of our own bodies. What if we applied the same the logic to the body of Christ? What if we were hyper-vigilant about the state of the body of Christ? There are wounds, there is ongoing probability of more injury—we Christians are lovers in dangerous times. The body of Christ is not safe or well—and one of the jobs of the preacher (as a pastoral presence in a particular location) is to monitor the health of the body. This is about context, and having a clear understanding of the harm that has been done in a particular congregation, as well as the risk of harm continuing. The preacher pays attention to the well-being of the whole body of Christ.

It is interesting to reflect on the body of Christ as a being in the world. It is so large and diverse that it can hardly be measured or defined, at least not in a global sense. It is perhaps easier to see the wounds than it is to see the whole. We can only get a grasp on the health of the body of Christ in limited contexts—like congregations, or denominations, or regions. So perhaps the question ought to be, what do healthy, functioning communities look like? Like the risen Christ, even functioning communities will be plagued by wounds and brokenness. They are fluid and dynamic and hard to pin down to monitor health and well-being. The body is not perfect, even in its most authentic form. The church, as the body of Christ in the world, is messy and always being renewed. Perhaps an authentic church is one that submits itself to renewal, a continual reconfiguration of trauma and grace. This kind of re-creation is what we yearn for in our individual, physical bodies. A functioning body of Christ is sustained by water and Spirit.

Preaching reminds us that we belong to God through our baptism in Jesus Christ. That is the situation of the body—located within a circle of divine grace, animated by love. The next section turns to the importance of remembering baptism. It is within the community of the baptized body that we find the fullest expression of belonging.

## REMEMBERING OUR BAPTISMS: THE MEMORY OF LOVE'S REFRAIN

The great American singer-songwriter Nat King Cole had a song that haunted his dreams, the memory of a time when he was together with his beloved. All that love, now gone, is the "stardust" of yesterday. What remains is the "memory of love's refrain"—a memory of sweetness and connection that comes to gently haunt the present. A memory of what it means to be loved and loving, a memory of wholeness. For several weeks I was haunted by the melody of that old tune "Stardust," struck by the beauty of that line: "the memory of love's refrain." Baptism is a refrain of love that echoes through our lives of faith. Baptism carries within it the seeds of remembrance—an invitation to remember who we are and to whom we belong. We remember that we are creatures of the creator—designed in the image of God, offered complete freedom through baptism. We remember not only the event of the baptism but its continuing effect—by water we are joined to others to create a living body that moves and breathes and suffers and celebrates. The body of Christ is incarnate, vulnerable, dynamic—it is alive in every sense of the word.

Baptism is an initiation rite in which water is sprinkled over a person's head or they are immersed fully in water. It signifies the coming of the Holy Spirit and a person's dying and rising to new life in Christ. It is a symbolic act with real material consequences. My tradition baptizes infants, and we see relatively few adult baptisms. One of the pitfalls of baptizing small children is that they are unlikely to remember the event itself. They will rely on the stories of others to tell them whether they cried or who was present on the day. When my children were small, they had photos of their baptisms in their bedrooms—so that they would be daily reminded that they are baptized. Preaching that affirms is also preaching that remembers baptism as the central identity that shapes ethics for Christians. In other words, baptism determines the way we behave toward each other in the church. Preaching is a means to communicate the gospel of baptismal grace that will determine the functioning of the body.

This section brings together baptism and sexuality in critical theological reflection. Baptismal promises have been broken in terms of the church's response to sexual difference, damaging the unity and well-being of the body. How might the body be re-membered? Baptismal identity renews our imagination toward an embrace of all sexual identities and offers healing hope for a broken community. Bathed in the waters of baptism, we are set free to begin to heal and reconnect the broken pieces. As we shall see, the waters of baptism prepare us for relationship with one another in the church and beyond. Baptism creates a community of belonging. Unfortunately, the community has often rejected even those who have been initiated by the waters of baptism.

## The Body of Christ

### BAPTISMAL IDENTITY AND CONNECTION

In baptism, each individual body is welcomed into a shared body—the body of Christ. I don't want to lose sight of individual bodies amid the collective, because individual bodies matter. They form the component parts of the embodied Christ. Individual bodies are beloved and valuable. We retain our individuality even as we are joined together with others. In baptism, we are named as those who have been loved before we were even born. We are made welcome in all our various identities. Baptism offers a distinctive posture of belonging, rooted in Jesus' own baptism, ministry, death, and resurrection. Too often, however, queer people are excluded from this core Christian posture and so barred from full inclusion in the life of discipleship. Elizabeth Stuart argues that in baptism we belong to another world, that our other identities do not determine our worth or value in God's eyes.[18]

> Heterosexuality and homosexuality and maleness and femaleness are not of ultimate importance, they are not determinative in God's eyes and in so far as any of us have behaved as if they are, we are guilty of the grave sin of idolatry, and if we have further behaved as if they are grounds upon which to exclude people from the glorious liberty of the children of God, we are guilty of profanity and a fundamental denial of our own baptismal identity which rests in being bound together with others not of our choosing by an act of sheer grace.[19]

In other words, when we exclude people from full expression of their sexual identities, we are denying our own baptismal identity. There is also a sense in which we are breaking our baptismal promises.

---

18. Stuart, "Sacramental Flesh," 68.
19. Stuart, "Sacramental Flesh," 68.

## BROKEN BODY, BROKEN PROMISES

> In baptismal liturgies, the gathered community represents the whole Body of Christ and makes promises to the person being baptized. What are the responsibilities of the baptized body towards the one who is baptized? According to this liturgy from the Church of Scotland's book of Common Order, participants promise to welcome and live in a "kindly and Christian way."[20] You who are gathered here Represent the whole Church, The Church catholic. Word and Sacrament bring you
> The joy of Christ's presence in your midst. They also bring you responsibilities. As Christ's people in this place.
> Do you welcome ____;
> And do you renew your commitment, With God's help, To live before all God's children in a kindly and Christian way, And to share with them
> The knowledge and love of Christ?[21]

The Christian Reformed Church offers a different congregational vow that specifically focuses on "oneness."

> Joyfully we receive you into the body of Christ.
> Join with us as we give witness in the world to the good news, for we are all one in Christ Jesus. Alleluia.[22]

The CRC formulation speaks powerfully of the inclusion into Christ's body as oneness. What are we promising when we stand up as Christians at the initiation of a new Christian? What are the limits of those promises? What does it mean for individuals to be one with each other? I usually tell congregations that they are signing a blank check when they baptize a person—they are saying that whatever that person needs—emotionally, spiritually, materially—that the church will show up and care for its own member. This promise constitutes a distinct ethic—a recognition of interdependence and a willingness to provide the necessities of life to

---

20. *Book of Common Order*, 92.
21. *Book of Common Order*, 92.
22. CRC, "Service for Baptism."

support members of the body. Through the exclusion and lack of care shown to LGBTQ people, Christian community has broken its baptismal promises.

Lauren Winner has written about the dangers of Christian practice, and the propensity for practices to be exploited or deformed. "Because nothing created is untouched by the Fall, Christians should not be surprised when lovely and good, potentially gracious Christian gestures are damaged, or when human beings deploy those Christian gestures in the perpetuation of damage."[23] It would take several books to write about the damage that has been accomplished by preaching. It has, for example, been plagued by anti-Judaism in its scriptural and theological interpretations. Baptism, for example, has been used most horrifically throughout the history of the church to forcefully baptize individuals without their choice or consent.[24] We know that the history of the Eucharist has been exclusive, for example, and tends to allow some and not others to be present at the table. Denominations have behaved as though it were up to humanity to decide who belongs at Christ's table, rather than being solely the invitation of Jesus. If we are alert to the kinds of characteristic damage that takes place in sacraments, we may be able to prevent such damage in the future.[25] It is Christian community that falters when our core practices are deformed—"When our theologies do not align with the core practices of Christian life, our imaginations about our neighbours' identities become distorted."[26] We do damage in baptism when we fail to love and affirm people in all their identities, or when queer people are rejected altogether. For example, it is a failure of a baptismal ethic of hospitality when we refuse to use a person's chosen pronouns and/or name.

Once we have faced the damage of our practices, we can lament the harm they have caused, and we can ask God to

---

23. Winner, *Dangers of Christian Practice*, 3.
24. Winner, *Dangers of Christian Practice*, 96.
25. Winner, *Dangers of Christian Practice*, 155.
26. Barton, *Becoming the Baptized Body*, 27.

repair the damage and participate in all the ways available to us as human agents.[27]

## THE BAPTIZED BODY

Disability theologian Sarah Barton uses the term "the baptized body" to speak of "the group of people inextricably caught up in one another by nature of their baptism into Jesus' death and resurrection life."[28] She argues that a baptismal hermeneutic can enliven the practice and imagination of the church when it responds to persons with disabilities. "Baptismal theologies and practice, sites of radical affirmation of the profound interdependence of human persons on Jesus Christ and the community of Jesus' body, as well as a deeply embodied and Spirit-enabled participation in discipleship, are critical for the renarration of Christian identity in contemporary churches."[29] What Barton is proposing, a baptismal hermeneutic, provides an intriguing direction for preaching that affirms. Barton suggests that Paul's theology of baptism was oriented around Jesus, participation, and community.[30] In addition, she argues that Paul has rooted his understanding of baptismal identity in the flourishing of people across difference.[31]

Each child, each adult that desires baptism is a desired child of God—chosen and loved. One of my favorite liturgical practices is to speak these words while holding the gaze of a child or adult being baptized:

> For you, Jesus Christ came into the world:
> For you he lived and showed God's love;
> For you he suffered the darkness of Calvary
> And cried at the last "It is accomplished";

27. Winner, *Dangers of Christian Practice*, 160.
28. Barton, *Becoming the Baptized Body*, 191.
29. Barton, *Becoming the Baptized Body*, 13. There are strong connections between disability and queer theologies—persons with disabilities and queer people have faced similar barriers to belonging in the Christian community.
30. Barton, *Becoming the Baptized Body*, 103.
31. Barton, *Becoming the Baptized Body*, 103.

## The Body of Christ

For you he triumphed over death and rose in newness of life;
For you he ascended to reign at God's right hand.
All this he did for you, though you do not know it yet.
And so the word of Scripture is fulfilled:
"we love because God loved us first."[32]

It is the simplest of arguments. We love because we have been loved. Loved in such a manner that we are prepared to welcome and include others, to care for the body with which we have been entrusted. It is as baptized Christians that we come to the tasks of confession, weeping, and resistance. Our confession of sin comes on the heels of our confession that God is great and merciful. Our lament arises because we know that we as human beings cannot fix this mess. Our resistance emerges out of a commitment to let the gospel loose in the world.

---

32. *Book of Common Order*, 90.

# 3

# Preaching That Weeps, Confesses, and Resists

### REMEMBERING RIGHTLY

My academic institution has struggled to respond to denominational debates over sexuality. As a theological college of the Presbyterian Church in Canada, its practice is to follow the course set by the denomination's General Assembly. For many years, the college was dominated by silence on the matters of human sexuality and LGBTQ affirmation, mirroring denominational silence. As the denomination has become more affirming, the college realized that the time for silence had come to an end, and we were ready to begin a new conversation. In this period of reflection and conversation, I began to examine my own practices. Despite serving as the minister of the chapel for a decade, never did I explicitly welcome or name the presence of LGBTQ members of the community. Recently, I led the following call to worship at our weekly chapel service:

> Whatever your past or your future
> Whatever the shade of your skin
> Whatever language comes most naturally . . . you belong here.

## Preaching That Weeps, Confesses, and Resists

If you are LGBTQ or however you identify, you belong here. If you are too young or too old, you belong here. If you are not sure if you belong, you belong here. This is God's house, this is worship. And we were born for this.

This was the first time in the history of the college, as far as I know, that LGBTQ folks were explicitly integrated into the worship experience. I was intentional with my words, but I could not have anticipated the response they elicited. One student explained that it was like the words were tiny angels that moved through the chapel, scattering the clouds of gloom that had hung for so long. Speaking those words—such simple words—was an act of recognition that allowed the community to remember its own diversity. It was like a breath of fresh air. My only regret was that I hadn't spoken these words sooner. I didn't know that they needed to be spoken. For years, I was oblivious to the unspoken grief and sense of exclusion that permeated the walls of my institution because of the wounds caused to the whole community by sexuality debates. My call to worship was a tiny step toward healing. Once those words were spoken out loud, they were set loose in the community to bring new life. They inspired a whole series of necessary conversations. One of those conversations is about the harm that has been done to the entire body of Christ because of the exclusion of queer folks. That harm, which was recounted in the previous chapter, constitutes a need for confession on the part of the whole church.

Before any process of reconciliation can occur, there must be a process of remembering rightly. Before we can heal, we must take the time to recount the injury that has been done and to take note of the wounds that remain. As we have learned from the Truth and Reconciliation processes in places such as South Africa and Canada, reconciliation is not possible until truth is told. Before we can get to affirmation, we must confess our sins and apologize to those we have harmed. They say confession is good for the soul. It is also good for the community. It is vital that we name the damage out loud, as well as our commitment to repair and healing. This confession results in release from guilt and shame for perpetrators and an opportunity to respond differently in the future. This section examines weeping and confession as they relate to preaching and sexuality.

## PREACHING AS WEEPING AND CONFESSION

In her groundbreaking work *Preaching as Weeping, Confession and Resistance: Radical Responses to Radical Evil,* Christine M. Smith names preaching as a theological act. Preachers are working theologians who engage in an act of theological naming.[1]

> The naming of reality functions in many ways, but whether naming calls persons to claim the fullness of their own created worth and the worth of all creation, or whether naming enables the demonic powers of hatred and injustice to be exposed and dethroned, one can hardly dispute the power of publicly proclaimed words . . . It is an act of disclosing and articulating the truth about our present human existence. It is an act of bringing new reality into being, and act of creation. It is also an act of redeeming and transforming reality, an act of shattering illusions and cracking open limited perspectives. It is nothing less than the interpretations of our present world and an invitation to build a profoundly different world.[2]

Smith names realities such as sexism, ageism, classism, ableism, and heterosexism as radically evil oppressions. She ponders similar questions to those I posed in an earlier section.

> Why has it taken me this many years to give the name "radical evil" to this web of oppressive structures and systems? I have understood these systems and ideologies as expressions of injustice, as sources of immense

---

1. Smith, *Preaching as Weeping*. Now three decades old, this book reflects the terminology of its time, such as "gay men and lesbian women" and "homosexuals."

2. Smith, *Preaching as Weeping*, 2.

suffering, even as demonic repercussions of human greed, fear, and hatred. It is only at this stage in my life, somewhat overwhelmed and enraged at the magnitude of the reality that confronts us, that I can no longer name this complex reality as anything but evil.[3]

It is important to note the emphasis is on evil systems, not evil individuals, although individuals, communities, or subcommunities may align themselves with a particular systemic evil. I am similarly naming any theology that seeks to oppress, erase, marginalize, or hate LGBTQ persons to be a manifestation of systematic evil.

Each person and community has a unique theological fingerprint. Each of us carry an eclectic set of beliefs that align to a greater or lesser extent with a faith tradition. For example, I am a Presbyterian. My personal beliefs are generally aligned with my denomination's doctrine, but I have been influenced by my encounters with theologies beyond the Reformed tradition. There are other reasons my theology is unique, such as my identity, my experience of God, my approach to Scripture, and my geographic, cultural, and economic locations. How we name God, how we understand human beings and the nature of the church, what we believe about sin and salvation—all of these will differ slightly from person to person, church to church. Of course, we overlap with one another in significant ways, forming communal beliefs—in families, in congregations, in nations, in cultures. It is quite remarkable to think about a particular congregation in terms of its theological diversity. In each community, there will be some who are victims of radical evil, some who participated willingly in it, others who are unknowingly caught up in webs of oppression. All of this results in considerable diversity of theology, and significant variation in how those theologies are practiced and expressed. The challenge, of course, is that we preach to everyone all at once.

Smith names the tasks of homiletics as weeping, confession, and resistance. Together, these terms provide a rich opportunity to reflect on the practice and ethics of the homiletic task, which

3. Smith, *Preaching as Weeping*, 3.

Smith sees as a redemptive activity in the face of radical evil. In conversation with Smith, I will explore what weeping, confession, and resistance might look like in terms of preaching human sexuality. Smith's terminology is dated, but the analysis of evil systems and the homiletic response remains one of the most helpful homiletic proposals of the last thirty years. Smith writes about preaching as a kind of passionate weeping, in which those who preach "need to engage their deepest passions, their highest values, their surest convictions and make them present and alive in moments of proclamation."[4] Preaching as weeping, however, calls forth pain and rage, not only the deep passion of which Smith writes. In terms of sexuality, Smith notes that lives of gay men and lesbian women are violated and endangered in the name of the Christian gospel. The church provides a theological and biblical foundation for the oppression of sexual minorities. This oppression must be named and confessed.

Smith wonders how the act of confession would function differently in liturgical settings if it were perceived as profound truth-telling: "Hope is engendered by the truth."[5] "In the act of preaching we strive to speak the truth about life in the perpetual belief and abiding hope that such truth, as devastatingly ugly and frighteningly beautiful as it is, is precisely what we bring to be offered, blessed, and transformed by God in the sacred act of preaching."[6] The truth about the treatment of queer people in the church is indeed devastatingly ugly. There is, of course, beauty intertwined with the not-so-pretty—there is grace and friendship. In preaching, we name all these things. It will be deeply painful to name the damage—for the preacher and for the listener. Healing, however, begins with the naming of reality—in the case of preaching, with a public naming of reality. This public naming may also be called confession, and we now turn to an examination of confession regarding harm done to LGBTQ communities.

---

4. Smith, *Preaching as Weeping*, 4.
5. Smith, *Preaching as Weeping*, 4.
6. Smith, *Preaching as Weeping*, 5.

## CONFESSING THE HARM

North American denominations are at different places when it comes to the full inclusion of LGBTQ people. Even while they continue to wrestle with the theology of sexuality and its practice, most are aware that there has been significant wounding to the Christian community throughout the history of the church and the course of the debates about human sexuality. A faithful response is to make a confession or an apology to those who have been harmed. I have chosen to share the Confession of my own denomination, because it is the one with which I am most familiar and most closely aligned.

The 2022 General Assembly adopted a confession to God and LGBTQ people, confessing the harm caused by homophobia, transphobia, heterosexism, and hypocrisy in the Presbyterian Church in Canada and committing the church to a true change of heart and behavior. The whole church is called to live out this confession as individuals and communities of faith so that harm does not continue.

> THE MEANING OF CONFESSION
> This confession is addressed to God and to each other
> in the presence of the whole community of believers.
> It presupposes the existence of a breach, or a falling short,
> that runs contrary to God's desire
> for how people live with and treat each other.
> It calls the church: to acknowledge harms done;
> to seek forgiveness from God and those who have been harmed;
> to stop causing harm; to repent of wrongdoing;
> and to begin a new journey of reparation, restoration, and reconciliation
> within the community of believers.
>
> OUR CONFESSION TO GOD AND LGBTQI PEOPLE
> All: Let us pray.
> One: In response to the Holy Spirit's action in its midst
> The Presbyterian Church in Canada comes before God
> in the presence of one another
> to confess its sins to God, and to LGBTQI people.

The church has wounded many
through its practices of exclusion and hurtful treatment.
The church seeks your forgiveness, O God,
and the forgiveness of all whom we have harmed.
All: We offer this confession in humility, desiring to go a new way.
One: Creating and Covenanting God,
you created us in your own image.
In Christ, you call us to be a welcoming and nurturing community,
to love one another as Christ has loved us.
Yet we have ostracized and excluded LGBTQI people
from full life within the body of Christ.
We have often turned the courts of the church into places
where those who are not straight or cisgender
are attacked, shunned and belittled.
We confess that we have failed
to love one another as Christ commanded us
and we have disrupted our covenantal relationship with you.
All: For these wrongful and unjust actions, we ask forgiveness.
One: The church has enacted policies and adopted customs
that have dehumanized and harmed LGBTQI people.
In doing so the church has led many people to believe
they have to choose between
embracing their sexuality and gender identity
or being a part of the church.
All: For these wrongful and unjust actions, we ask forgiveness.
One: The church has often perpetuated
harmful lies that LGBTQI people are dangerous and abusive.
The resulting stigma fosters an environment
where gifted people are discouraged and excluded
from providing leadership in the church.
The church's prejudice contributes to
hatred and neglect of LGBTQI people
making them targets for physical, spiritual and emotional violence.
All: For these unloving and unjust actions, we ask forgiveness.
One: The church has no higher calling
than to offer the worship that belongs to God.
In worship, we find strength and hope
for proclaiming God's reign in the world.
Yet often our language in worship is not inclusive
and renders many people and their families invisible.

This makes worship
a wounding and alienating experience.
All: For these unloving and unjust actions, the church asks forgiveness.
One: The church has been dismissive of and indifferent to
LGBTQI people when they have named
the harm the church has caused
to their mental, physical and spiritual well-being.
All: For these unloving and unjust actions, we ask forgiveness.
One: O God of justice and mercy,
you have called us to love and nurture the vulnerable among us,
yet we have not been loving and supportive role models
to young LGBTQI people.
We have failed to listen to their cries for healthy pastoral support.
Our actions have abandoned them to a future
that often includes internalized homophobia, self-loathing, depression,
substance abuse, self-harm, homelessness, and suicide.
All: For these unloving and unjust actions, we ask forgiveness
One: In this church called home,
some LGBTQI people still long
for the love and security of home.
In this church called home,
some of us have witnessed
demeaning conversations and attitudes
that belittle LGBTQI people.
Yet we choose to be silent in the face of such injustices,
becoming complicit in the resulting oppression.
All: For these unloving and unjust actions, we ask forgiveness.
One: Creating God,
your creation bears witness
to the vastness of your diversity.
In carrying out the mission entrusted to it,
the church has embraced ideologies and narratives
that have normalized the exclusion
of those it deems different.
All: For these unloving and unjust actions, we ask forgiveness.
One: To those of you whom we have harmed
by our unloving and unjust actions,
we confess that we have failed you.
We acknowledge that the church has wounded you deeply.

All: In humility and with sorrow, we ask for your forgiveness.
One: Come Holy Spirit come.
Be present in this time of silence.
(Hold a moment of silence)
One: God of justice and mercy,
we praise you for the presence of the Holy Spirit
prompting us to work
purposefully and compassionately,
to find new and just ways
of living out that larger story
of loving God and neighbour.
Help us to overcome
the pride that covers up wrongdoings,
the indifference that stands in the way of feeling,
and the fear that stalls change.
All: God of justice and mercy, we turn to you.
Only you can help us to do this hard work
of repairing, restoring, reconciling and healing.
Fill us with courage and hope
as we commit to working
for the restoration of your church and
our relationship with one another, and
for the collective flourishing of all people
for your glory.
All: Amen.[7]

This Confession marked an important step towards healing in my denomination. By making such a confession, the church made a commitment to protect LGBTQ folks in the future and continue to examine its own beliefs and perspectives. While this confession is a tremendously positive move, it falls short in several ways. The confession is aimed at the LGBTQ community, but it fails to account for the ways that heterosexual people, indeed, the whole church has been harmed. We often talk about the reality of exclusion as if it targets only the LGBTQ members of a community. But the entire community is diminished when certain members are excluded or undervalued. Non-affirming theologies and biblical interpretations hurt the entire church. The analogy of the body is helpful. We

7. PCC, "Confession to God and LGBTQI People."

understand intuitively that the parts of our body are connected to each other. If one part of you is hurting, it affects all the other parts. If you have a headache, it might make you sick to your stomach or cause your eyes to become sensitive. The same is true of the body of Christ. If one parts suffers, all parts suffer together.

Another reality that must be confessed is the division that has been caused by debates over human sexuality. We are designed to be a body—united even though we disagree. However, the church has been shattered by division, possibly because it is very difficult to compromise on issues of sexuality. There has been a lack of respectful conversation. There has been anger and condescension. I have listened to individuals intentionally using the term "brothers and sisters" as a weapon that excludes trans and non-binary folks who do not identify with either category. I have heard views of theology that are so opposite to my understanding that one wonders if we are reading the same Bible. I have found myself avoiding certain individuals because I am so appalled by their beliefs about sexuality. These are extreme examples. Most often, we are alienated from one another in more subtle ways—unable to have conversations about sexuality because we fear there will be disagreement. The body of Christ is diverse, and this diversity forms part of its beauty. Disagreement is inevitable and simply a consequence of variety—we are different, and we will comprehend our lives, and God's life, in various ways. The disagreement is not the problem. The problem is when the body is torn apart because of disagreement. In many denominations, congregations are leaving because of decisions that have been made. Congregations and other faith communities are divided within themselves. It is this dismemberment of the body of Christ that must be confessed—our failure to remain in relationship with one another. A body does not function well when it is missing parts. We share agency with the Holy Spirit to maintain the health of the body. The church has failed at maintaining the safety and unity-in-diversity of the body of Christ.

All these actions and inactions can be named from the pulpit as wounds experienced by the body of Christ. Preachers simply point to the wounds and acknowledge that there is harm done.

There is no need to blame any one person—the failure to maintain safety and unity-in-diversity is a shared failure. We confess the harm that the body of Christ has done to itself by failing to listen deeply enough or engage in conversation with those who hold different theologies, or by actively trying to exclude and marginalize LGBTQ people. By pointing to the wounds, we draw attention to the suffering rather than focusing on those who have perpetrated the suffering. Denominational confessions and apologies are helpful for preaching in this context because they represent shared confession—the confession of the whole church, which includes LGBTQ people. While some have caused more damage than others, and some have been injured more than others, our confession belongs to the body of Christ as a whole.

## ASSURANCE OF PARDON

Sermons that confess our corporate sin should also remind us that we are forgiven for our sins. In Christian liturgy the assurance of pardon immediately follows the prayer of confession. This immediacy is instructive about the way that God forgives—there is a sense in which God stands ready to forgive the moment our confession leaves our mouths. The assurance of pardon is a reminder that we are forgiven by God and made free in Jesus Christ, no matter what we have done or what we have left undone. Our confession carries an implicit promise that we will stop what we were doing and change direction. The assurance of pardon assumes that one can occupy the future in a different way than in the past—change is possible. To confess is to resist the claim that change is not possible, the claim that once we are blemished we are forever blemished. When we confess to God and to one another we are claiming instead that it is possible for harm to cease and be transformed. We are hopeful that those we have wronged will receive our confession and respond in such a way that allows us to move forward in relationship.

Our confession to God is made with the certainty that we will receive grace and mercy. Our confession to our neighbor holds no such assurance. People are slower than God when it comes to forgiveness. Our neighbor may or may not be willing to hear and receive what we have to say. It matters, however, that the words are spoken, that the confession is made, even if it will not necessarily be welcomed.

Confession and assurance of pardon are not one-time events. We repeat them as often as we worship together, because our sin is ongoing and our need for forgiveness is continual. It is not enough for denominations to make public confessions once and hope that relationships will be healed. Rather, confession for the ill-treatment of queer communities will need to be repeated if it is to influence our shared life. Preaching offers an opportunity to repeatedly confess the damage and receive the good news that the harm need not continue. There is a pathway to healing and wholeness. Our confession implies that we will try to prevent pain in the future, leading to a need for resistance against structures of sin.

## PREACHING AS RESISTANCE

Preaching gently and respectfully names the wounds of the church and confesses the behaviors and attitudes that have caused the wounds. Sermons offer a way forward, a way to heal the wounds. To heal, preaching must take sides. It must choose whether it will stand on the side of the oppressed or the oppressor. Resistance is taking a stand against evil from the pulpit. "If preaching is to be a transforming act, then the power and integrity of our proclamation will surely be measured by their ability to mobilize communities to resist the reality that confronts us."[8] In the case of this book, I am arguing that preachers need to develop capacity to mobilize communities to resist the oppressive structures of homophobia/transphobia and heteronormativity. Resistance will involve taking a stance against homophobic perspectives on human sexuality as revealed in Scripture and prevalent within the human community. If we confess homophobia and transphobia as sins, then we must

8. Smith, *Preaching as Weeping*, 5.

also offer an alternative perspective that is more aligned with God's movement toward us. It will also involve taking a stand against heteronormativity as it appears in our daily lives. That is, most of us are accustomed to relationships between men and women and will likely assume that experience to be normative. Instead, we are invited to make space for other kinds of relationships reflected in LGBTQ experience. It is challenging to rethink what is familiar and "normal"; for example, by rethinking marriage as something that happens between two people rather than only between a man and a woman. We can resist heteronormativity by confessing the reality that we operate as though heterosexism is normative and everything else derivative.

Ginger Gaines-Cirelli has generated a compelling vision for sacred resistance, not as a discrete action but as a way of being in the world—a stance or posture. Centered on God, this posture resists all that is not God.[9] It is sacred because it is not self-focused but rather because "it is God who inspires our action, sustains our action, and provides the ultimate vision that is the goal of our action."[10] Ultimately, our resistance is grounded in the prophetic traditions of Scripture that find their fulfillment in Jesus Christ. Sacred resistance, says Gaines-Cirelli, "is anything—any word, deed, or stance—that actively counters the forces of hatred, cruelty, selfishness, greed, dehumanization, desolation, and disintegration in God's beloved world."[11] Sermons can adopt a stance of sacred resistance against homophobic and transphobic theologies. Most of us are accustomed to taking a stance of sacred resistance against other dangerous theologies and perspectives. After all, the gospel that we preach critiques church and world. Our individual and collective sin is named and confronted in sermons. This sinfulness—woundedness—is met with grace. That grace itself compels us to resist those things that harm the community. Some will ask whether it is appropriate for preachers to "take sides"—it is appropriate for the preacher to speak against those behaviors and

---

9. Gaines-Cirelli, *Sacred Resistance*, loc. 195.
10. Gaines-Cirelli, *Sacred Resistance*, loc. 208.
11. Gaines-Cirelli, *Sacred Resistance*, loc. 358.

attitudes which harm LGBTQ people and the entire Christian community. As Gaines-Cirelli argues:

> Jesus had to choose a stance and Jesus chose a side. It wasn't the side of the status quo. It wasn't the side of the strong and powerful. It wasn't the side of personal comfort or cheap grace. It wasn't the side of self-protection or revenge. It wasn't the side of wealth or privilege. Jesus chooses the underside, the outside, the pushed-aside. He stands on the side of justice, he stands on the side of self-giving love, and he stands on the side of humility and vulnerability. Jesus doesn't choose the side of the poor and oppressed because he loves only them. Jesus takes that side because he loves all people and knows that "when one part of the body suffers, the whole body suffers with it."[12]

To choose a side, to stand with the LGBTQ community, is to stand against oppressive theologies. Our resistance against oppressive theologies will be offensive to some within the community of faith. What does this mean in practical terms? We preach to the entire diverse gathering, regardless of how they express their identities and theologies. We as preachers are always invited to take the side of the gospel (however we might interpret that word). This entails a yes to gospel and a no to the powers that suppress gospel news. Those who choose to align themselves with anti-gospel forces—hatred, anger, homophobia/transphobia—may feel attacked or rejected for their views. This cannot be helped. We run the risk of alienating certain of our members. This kind of truth-telling is offensive as it tells a terrible story of mistreatment and hate. It is offensive because it calls our behavior and ethics into question. Some of our listeners will not be ready for this conversation, and that must be acceptable. Sermons that proclaim a positive vision for human sexuality are intended to be good news for everyone. It is good news when we are confronted with the limitations of our behavior and invited on a path toward change. Over time, the hope

---

12. Gaines-Cirelli, *Sacred Resistance*, loc. 1840.

is that preaching will equip listeners with skills and perspectives that allow for new possibilities.

It is difficult to know how to respond to those who have been party to communal confessions yet choose to continue the harm. Although my denomination made this confession as a body, there are individuals who have decided that it does not apply to them. They have said "sorry" but have not altered their behavior or attitudes. Despite acknowledging the injury done to LGBTQ persons, some preachers continue to claim faithfulness to homophobic/transphobic theologies. Thus, we return to the subject of weeping. The struggle for equity and fairness is a long struggle, and many of us will grieve the continued damage to queer communities wrought by preachers with destructive theologies.

One of the goals of this book, taken up in the next chapter, is the healing of division within the church. Readers may wonder how churches can heal from division when I am naming certain theologies as problematic. We are accustomed to a more conciliatory and tolerant approach that "doesn't judge other people's theology." One of the questions that has plagued me is: "How can I, as an advocate for inclusion, make space to include even those with different theological perspectives?" For inclusion to be real, it must include those with radically different viewpoints. It need not, however, be hospitable to homophobic or transphobic theologies. When these theologies are encountered, they must be resisted. There is endless room for wondering, for questioning, for conversation about sexuality and theology. There is room for negative perceptions and/or myths about human sexuality—room for ignorance and lack of experience. But there is no room for hatred or disrespect within the body of Christ.

Preachers critically examine the theologies that sustain the church. We are painfully aware of how the church historically has used theology to hurt certain populations. The history of the Christian church is inextricably bound up in colonialism, for example. Drawing on various Scriptures, the church erroneously painted a theological picture that justified the oppression and murder of millions of people. In Canada, this resulted in the deaths of thousands of Indigenous children and the suffering of countless others. These children were removed from their homes and communities and placed in residential institutions that were charged with removing their heritage, language, and familial ties. The Presbyterian Church in Canada was one of several denominations that participated in this violent and abusive task of removing Indigenous children from their families. The Presbyterian Church in Canada has apologized for its behavior and its attitudes that encouraged "civilizing mission"—the belief that only white people are civilized and that all others should be shaped and formed in the image of white people (white men). Our public confession to Indigenous peoples, made in 1994, implied a commitment to stop any behavior or attitude that would cause similar harm.[13] The confession of homophobia/transphobia should be no different. Once we are aware of how a particular theology has been misused to cause harm to certain populations, that theology should no longer be preached in the church. Those who continue to preach homophobic/transphobic theologies are causing further harm to the body of Christ. Unfortunately, such preaching will continue. Those of us who find ourselves in an affirming position will need to speak loudly and clearly both in opposition to theologies of exclusion, and in favor of theologies that more adequately express the fullness of God's love.

It will be necessary for the preacher to engage in a process of deconstructing the homophobic/transphobic and heteronormative theologies that have dominated in the church for a long time. To combat exclusionary theologies, we must understand the arguments for and against inclusion, including the positions of those with whom we vehemently disagree. Rather than merely demolishing homophobic/transphobic or heteronormative theologies we can engage in a more constructive project of building up the body of Christ. Preachers can cast a vision for what the body of Christ can look like when it is whole and healthy. Those who lean towards exclusive views are given an alternative way of being. They are invited to lay aside hatred in favor of more life-giving postures—such

13. PCC, "Confession Indigenous."

as curiosity, generosity, and hospitality. While preachers themselves must understand the various arguments, there is no need, for example, to rehearse the content of homophobic/transphobic theologies from the pulpit, or to pick apart theological arguments strand by strand. Instead, we can share a more positive vision for life together that is inclusive of all people.

## ENCOUNTERING OPPOSITION

One of my greatest fears as a preacher has nothing to do with the act of public speaking and everything to do with encountering negative responses to my sermon. When we line up to shake hands and bless each other at the door of the sanctuary, the conversation often turns to the sermon. While preachers know that the most common response is a simple "thank you" or "good sermon," occasionally we will be engaged in debate or be the recipient of a cutting remark. You can imagine that the conversations following a sermon that addresses sexuality might be challenging. While we imagine that church people are always good and kind, that is not the case, and preachers need to protect themselves as well as respond as graciously as possible without accepting spiritual violence or attack. It hurts to be confronted with opposition to sermons no matter what the subject or the reason. Each of us develop our own strategies for dealing with negative feedback. In the case of sexuality, as emotions run high, there is a distinct chance for harm or hurt to occur following the sermon. Preachers can be prepared for a variety of responses and perhaps even have answers at the ready. Obviously, the receiving line on the way out of church is not the place for deep theological discussion or debate. You might invite the person into further conversation on a more suitable occasion when there is time to speak in an unhurried manner. I encourage preachers to think through this scenario and imagine appropriate responses in their context. How can we both protect ourselves from attacks and make space for conversation?

Through weeping, confession, and resistance we tell the truth and seek to prevent further harm within the community. The next chapter considers the possibility of re-membering the body that has been broken by division and hatred. Preaching can heal the connective tissues that hold us together.

# 4

# Preaching a Gospel of Reconciliation

## UNTANGLING GOSPEL

My thumb hesitated over the retweet button, as I wondered whether to share the tweet from the Rev. Dr. Jacqui Lewis from Middle Church in New York City. "Homophobic and transphobic theologies are theologies of death. Period."[1] While every part of me agreed with her, I wondered whether I could say such a thing publicly, in the presence of colleagues with different perspectives. This led to a process of reflection and a lot of questions. If I am to be faithful to the gospel of Jesus Christ, then what must be my commitments? Should concern for upsetting my more conservative colleagues outweigh the responsibility I have to preach good news about human sexuality? As I described in the Introduction to this book, my fear of being challenged has made me reluctant to engage these issues in a public forum. At the same time, I value honest, respectful dialogue and do not want to shut down the possibility of conversation.

---

1. See https://twitter.com/RevJacquiLewis/status/1536348876831064065.

## Preaching a Gospel of Reconciliation

My commitment, theologically and otherwise, is to those who have suffered, been harmed, silenced, and excluded. Any theology that is homophobic or transphobic proclaims life to some, but not to all. Gospel is and must be good news for everyone. In the strange logic of the Spirit, what is good for the poor is also good for the rich. It might not sound like good news for the person who stands to lose power or wealth, but ultimately it is good news for everyone when vulnerable and marginalized communities are safe and raised up to new life. Any theology that excludes some from the fullness of God's grace is preaching a gospel of death, not life.

This book argues that preaching toward affirmation to reclaim the wholeness of the body is gospel news. However, such reclamation may not initially sound like good news. The gospel frequently sounds like bad news before it sounds like good news. Gospel calls on us to change, to repair, to confess, to include. Few of us will initially celebrate these kinds of transformations because they will demand something from us. Healing hurts. If we are to become more inclusive, for example, it involves shifting our position to make space for others. If we are to confess, we must come to terms with our own sinfulness. If we are to repair, it will cost us something. Preaching sermons that affirm will not always lead to generous feedback. They may instead lead to anger and self-righteousness. Transformation is a painful process, complicated by trauma and grief. This is especially true when the body being transformed is the collective body of the church. Gospel, however, promises God's presence and action amid transformation. The Holy Spirit is at work, giving us courage and flexibility as we engage in process of transformation. The gospel is ultimately good news because it directs us toward healing and hope, even if it first requires that we alter our behavior and attitudes.

Reconciliation is good news—it is gospel news. It will not initially sound like good news because it will require something from us regardless of where we find ourselves on the ideological or theological spectrum. It is difficult to imagine what healing and reconciliation might look like among those with divergent views on sexuality and faith. The intentional harm must be confessed, and it must cease before there is a possibility of reconciling. Reconciliation is not always desirable. Here the metaphor breaks down—for example, the body must be kept safe from predators and violent offenders. Symbolic unity is secondary to safety and security. The safety of the most vulnerable must always be paramount. Communities will need to make decisions about how they will protect spaces to make them as safe as possible for people of all sexual identities. Physical and emotional safety are prerequisites for reconciliation. The possibility of connection among a group of people when there is ongoing harm is greatly diminished. Harm reduction is necessary if a relationship is to be repaired. How do we reduce the danger and create safe spaces in our churches? Truthfully, I am not sure that any Christian space can ever be entirely safe because of the variety of beliefs that exist and our inability, or lack of desire, to control or police the space of worship and fellowship. Instead, we might ask what makes a community safer. Open dialogue and a spirit of respectful conversation, preaching that consistently and carefully constructs a positive vision for human sexuality, and an ethos of genuine concern for others within the community may contribute to safer spaces.

Gospel is also highly contextual—what is good news in one place may not be received with gladness elsewhere. Some churches and individuals will embrace LGBTQ persons and sexual diversity without requiring much change; others will require a much longer journey. Some churches will receive this kind of preaching as a blessed gift; others will receive it as an unwelcome intrusion to their familiar theologies. Some will leave the church or denomination altogether. We must preach the gospel, even if worship participants do not want to hear it.

Even though we will not always agree on the content or priorities of the gospel, preachers will benefit from becoming very clear about how they personally identify and proclaim gospel news. Preaching gospel may mean resisting the stance of "other gospels," which may be good news for some and not for others. To be honest, I'm not sure that non-affirming perspectives can be considered gospel because they cause injury. Those who preach against the wholeness of the body and the beautiful and complex sexuality of human beings do not seem to be preaching gospel. It may be good news for some, but not for all. Gospel, in my estimation, is always ultimately good news for everyone. When our systems are just and inclusive, we come closer to mirroring the divine love of the triune God. Our reflection of the divine is always imperfect, regardless of our theological stance. I do not mean to imply that those who hold affirming perspectives are better or more faithful people than those who are reluctant or opposed to full LGBTQ participation. I do, however, believe that affirming perspectives are more coherent with the gospel as it was preached and lived out by Jesus Christ. We are called to have compassion for those who have misunderstood the fierce and radical gospel that invites us to enlarge the table so that there is room for all.

All who have engaged in these theological conversations have been wounded and traumatized by the conversations themselves. There is hurt on all sides, although some wounds are deeper than others. The bulk of wounding has been experienced by LGBTQ people—the wounding cuts to the core of that community. More traditional individuals and congregations have also suffered from division and a sense of alienation from those who hold to less traditional theologies. My claim is that the church has been dismembered by these sexuality debates. Preaching can contribute to healing and reconciliation.

Each of us, regardless of our sexual identity, has sinned with our body in ways that cause harm to others and estrange us from God and neighbor—even from ourselves. Thus, our sin leads to estrangement and brokenness. It is safe to say that we have all hurt others, just as we have been hurt. No matter your sexual identity, if you are passionate about people and the church, you have likely been hurt at some point by the conversations you have had about sexuality and the church. The question is, can we move forward? Once the hurt has been named and confessed, can we move into a process of reconciliation among those parts of the body that have been separated? What is the role of preaching in reconciling the body of Christ that has been broken by painful attitudes and behavior?

Reconciliation is at the heart of the gospel, and a theme of preaching. What is reconciliation? Reconciliation happens when those who have been separated are brought back together. It does not necessarily imply friendship or intimacy, or even agreement. Rather, it is a mutual decision to offer respect and Christian love to the other party. Respect is honoring the other person's perspective, even if you disagree. To become affirming is a process of healing and reconciliation. The broken relationship between God and creation was repaired by the life, death, and resurrection of Jesus Christ. This is good news that is proclaimed in most sermons. We are reconciled to God and forgiven by God, which is gospel news. Even as we are reconciled to God in a deep and genuine way, reconciliation with other people remains incomplete, forgiveness elusive. Preaching proclaims the possibility of reconciliation and forgiveness within the human community—a space opened in the us/them binary that allows a spark of connection to flourish. Formed into one body, we are literally commanded to love one another. In fact, I would argue that the Bible spends far more time talking about how human beings should be reconciled to each other than it does talking about sexual relationships. Jesus came to build community, not just to save souls. It matters that we tend the connections between us particularly when the body is wounded by division.

## SAFE SPACE AND RECONCILIATION

As the minister of the chapel at my seminary, I have primary responsibility for community worship. We often have guest preachers, and generally they are sensitive to the ethos of the college. But one week during chapel we had a guest who, without warning, made a sweeping homophobic statement in the middle of his sermon. For many of us, it was an awkward and horrifying moment—we were hearing that homosexuality was the root of all evil in our culture. The faculty looked around at each other, wondering how to respond. No one felt they had the authority or the means to step in and heal the situation in some way. I sat there with my mouth hanging open, glancing anxiously around at queer students to check whether they were all right. In the end, we were unable to respond to the incident in the context of that worship service. A statement was issued after the event, but in the moment, the leadership was frozen. My point is that it is difficult to ensure safe space. Our guest preacher had not been adequately prepared for the theological atmosphere at the college, which is inclusive. This incident, while incredibly painful, presented an opportunity for us to think through the safety of our worshipping space. We realized that worship leaders needed to feel that they had authority to respond to hateful incidents when they arise. We realized that we needed to be much more vocal about our inclusive nature.

The worship space may never be entirely safe. LGBTQ people face the possibility of exclusion and rejection. Other people may find their boundaries pushed and their beliefs challenged. If it is not possible to ensure an entirely safe space for worship, what can we do to ensure adequate safety? We can pay attention to the safety of participants when queer bodies come into proximity with other bodies. We can have a clear boundary about what constitutes hate. In your context, what are the limits of faithful conversation? When does conversation degenerate into argument or hate speech? There must also be clear procedures for dealing with harm as it arises. Worship that includes both perpetrators and victims is uncomfortable. While some occupy the role of perpetrators of hurt, it may not be helpful to think of people this way—rather, to recognize that all have been damaged along the way, and many of our attitudes and behaviors about sexuality are deeply related to trauma. So, we acknowledge that all have fallen short—queer people and others.

Worship and preaching must be intended for the whole community, regardless of theological perspective or sexual identity. Those with traditional or conservative viewpoints worship side by side with progressive Christians. Those who have actively and vocally discriminated are seated next to those they have discriminated against. In the middle are all those who are unsure, whose opinions are unformed in this great debate about God's grace and who is deserving of that grace. Regardless of perspective, regardless of sexual identity, all are caught up in the great story of God's radical inclusive love. There is room for all at the table. But what does respectful dialogue look like? Are there times when some individuals should be excluded from the community because they are causing harm? What should we do, for example, with an aggressively anti-trans elder who is constantly harassing a young trans woman? Or what do we do with the lay leader whose prayers include the conversion of LGBTQ people? What about those who espouse and share homophobic theologies during coffee hour? How much harm will be allowed within the beloved community? What is our responsibility to protect the vulnerable and marginalized in our midst? There are more questions than answers when it comes to the concept of safe space.

Healing the body is a slow process and so very complex. We long for quick fixes, buying every product on the market to fix what ails us, and yet the one thing we cannot purchase is time. It takes time for learning to sink in. It takes time for cultures to change. It takes time to shape communities. It will take time to heal the parts of ourselves that have been wounded so that we can preach faithful sermons that honor not only our own sexuality but also that of others. We should avoid being prematurely celebratory. Reconciliation will take a great deal of hard work. While I am thrilled to witness congregations choosing to affirm all sexualities, I am slightly alarmed by the rainbows and balloons—are we celebrating too soon? Deciding to be affirming is one thing; acting it out is something different altogether. It is not reasonable, for example, to fly a Pride flag outside the church if the institution has not done the hard work of examining its own beliefs, biases, and interpretations of Scriptures. The potential for further damage is great if we claim to be affirming yet fail to protect those who are most vulnerable.

We must be modest about what can be achieved from the pulpit in terms of reconciliation. The most preachers can do is prepare listeners for this work of reconciliation that happens beyond the sanctuary. Preaching prepares us for life lived according to the gospel. The core of the gospel is that God reconciled us in Jesus Christ—to God and to our neighbor. We preach the miracle of God-with-us: that we have been reconciled to God, and that we have been shown how to live with our neighbor in a good way. Preaching proclaims the reality of reconciliation with God and the possibility of reconciliation with neighbor—both of which will be incomplete on this side of the eschaton. Reconciliation with our neighbors is an ongoing process that may require baby steps. A reconciled body will be loving and respectful, hospitable to all its parts.

## UNITY AND FORGIVENESS

For some, the unity of the body is paramount, and it is certainly a priority of the biblical witness. I confess to having been stung by the idea of unity, because it is often used as a weapon in sexuality debates. There has been, for example, conflict in my denomination because there is a tension between being hospitable to LGBTQ people and the presence of ethnic congregations who tend towards non-inclusive theologies.[2] There is a fear that we will lose the ethnic churches if the denomination becomes affirming and a perceived threat on the part of some congregations that they will indeed leave if queer folks are welcomed. Thus, there has been a decision to make—do we honor ethnic churches or do we honor LGBTQ people? Some have chosen unity with ethnic churches over unity with LGBTQ people, which results in the very disunity that has been feared. This situation raises questions about unity and what it means to maintain unity in the face of disagreement. There is a subtle, or not so subtle, implication that those with

---

2. The PCC has many congregations that are composed of a single nationality/ethnicity, including Korean, Chinese, Taiwanese, Ghanaian, Hungarian, and more. There is considerable theological diversity within and between these churches. Not all are non-affirming, but many have struggled mightily with the current affirming position of the Presbyterian Church in Canada.

marginalized sexual identities are causing division in the church. In my experience, those who were fighting for equality and inclusion were often accused of sowing the seeds of disunity. What do we do when unity requires the erasure of difference or enforced homogeneity? How can there be unity when some are not welcome at the table? Douglas John Hall writes:

> The unity that ought to characterize the Body of Christ is set over-against the militant and the subtle disunities, divisions and alienations that characterize human life under the conditions of historical existence. The dividing walls of hostility are being broken down; forgiveness and mutuality are being learned; reconciliation and *koinonia* are being experienced as real possibilities and not mere ideals. We are speaking here of the most central things of this faith.[3]

In other words, the body of Christ offers us a different pathway through our time-bound lives, not characterized by division but by forgiveness, mutuality, and community. Hall goes on:

> Oneness, in this tradition, is therefore not an ontic, static givenness but a dynamic mutuality that is glimpsed and struggled towards in the honest encounter of Creator with creature, and creature with creature. It is indeed the otherness of the other that makes such oneness necessary, but it is also the otherness of the other that makes such oneness possible. For the oneness desired by this gospel is the oneness of love, and love presupposes otherness even while it counters the alienation and estrangement that prevents love's realization.[4]

As a dynamic mutuality, oneness involves the continual struggle of encounter, as we tell our stories to each other. What we are struggling for is a oneness of love that counters estrangement. The gospel of Jesus Christ desires unity and fully engages difference.

---

3. Hall, "Church Beyond the Christian Religion."
4. Hall, "Church Beyond the Christian Religion."

> If the oneness of the church means that there is only one way of being the church, only one way of expressing Christian truth, only one way of living the Christian life, then this mark of the church must be considered one of the most oppressive of Christian teachings. Nothing could lend itself to totalitarian systems or authoritarian religions more readily than a unity-principle that permits of no plurality in its expression and realization.[5]

Unity cannot be forced; there must be plurality of opinion and expression. This is certainly true regarding sexuality. There is room for a wide range of opinions and expressions of those opinions. In a spirit of dynamic mutuality, we can be in conversation about our beliefs, our hopes, our identities. Each community will need to decide the limits of these conversations—are there expressions of belief that are not permitted in the assembly because they lead to the oppression of some members? Again, this is not about suppressing difference but preventing harm. Austin Hartke sums up the question of unity succinctly:

> There are two ways to interpret what Paul says in Galatians 3:28 about our being one in Christ: either it means that we're all whitewashed and homogenized and our differences are erased . . . or it means that we're called to find a way to make our different identities fit together, like bright shards in assorted colors that make up the stained glass windows of a cathedral. Are we called to sameness, or are we called to oneness?[6]

If reconciliation is a difficult path for churches divided on issues of sexuality, neither will we find an easy pathway to forgiveness. The damage that has been done cannot be undone. Confessions have been made, mistakes have been admitted, and perhaps denominations are beginning to recognize ways to heal the broken relationships. The possibility of forgiveness arises only once the intentional harm has stopped—it is not reasonable to ask for forgiveness while the injuries are ongoing. Forgiveness between

---

5. Hall, "Church Beyond the Christian Religion."
6. Hartke, *Transforming*, 169.

human beings is raised as a hope rather than a certainty. It is a profound and important hope that is rooted in the gospel of Jesus Christ. Bishop Desmond Tutu has argued that there is no future without forgiveness—that those existing on both sides of a conflict must find their way back together.[7] He believes that black and white South Africans are bound up together—their futures cannot be untangled.

> South Africans will survive and prevail only together, black, and white bound together by circumstance and history as we strive to claw our way out of the morass that was apartheid racism. Up and out together, black, and white together. Neither group on its own could or would make it. God had bound us, manacled us, together. In a way it was to live out what Martin Luther King, Jr., had said, "Unless we learn to live together as brothers [and sisters] we will die together as fools."[8]

In the future of the church and the body of Christ, our histories and futures are inextricably linked. Those who hold traditional views of sexuality and those with more progressive views—all are bound up together in the body. If we are going to continue to be the body of Christ, we rise and fall together.

As I write, it is difficult to imagine forgiveness in the context of sexuality debates. These debates have been so polarizing, and the body so damaged, that it is unclear whether the various sides can speak respectfully to each other on the topic of sexuality. If there is no respectful conversation, there can be no forgiveness, no reconciliation. While my denomination made a confession to LGBTQ communities, many preachers are still causing harm in their sermons by undermining the inherent value of queer folks. Congregations are leaving the denomination rather than abide by the decision of the church to be affirming. It may take lifetimes to repair the damage at the institutional level. Forgiveness at the congregational and individual level seems more likely. What role

---

7. Tutu, *No Future Without Forgiveness*.
8. Tutu, *No Future Without Forgiveness*, 8.

can sermons play in raising the possibility of forgiveness and facilitating stronger relationships among those in the pew?

## STRENGTHENING CONNECTIVE TISSUES

Once harm has been confessed and addressed, once the parties are in conversation, there arises the possibility of forgiveness and reconciliation. Confession is the easy part. Addressing the damage that has been done in concrete ways is a more difficult and lengthy process. This is a process of healing that begins with confession and then moves toward practical means of repair and reconciliation. What is the role of sermons in bringing about reconciliation within the body of Christ? Sermons can prepare us for relationship with each other by nurturing the connections between us and tending the wounds that are evident on the body. I hesitate to make too grand a claim for what preaching can accomplish in communities that are experiencing layers of pain and disconnection. We can be confident, however, that God is actively working to bring about new life in communities of faith that have suffered the pain and loss of conflict about sexuality. There are many examples of churches that have worked through the pain and found new life. In one circumstance with which I am familiar, a male pastor came out to his congregation and some were so unsettled that they left, only to return once they had an opportunity to reflect. Together, they worked through the challenges and ultimately became a stronger community, more accepting and affirming of all people.

Themes of reconciliation abound in Scripture, and a role of preaching is to encourage us to reconcile with God and with each other as we hear the same stories and are assured of the same promises. At the very least, sermons are a space in which we can have conversations about reconciliation and forgiveness. Preaching helps us to stay in conversation with each other by consistently reminding us of the need for reconciliation and forgiveness. Even when we cannot find the words to speak to each other face to face, we come together as a body to hear a message. We will have a thousand different recollections, perspectives, and theologies.

Filtered through our bodies, the preaching experience is unique to each one of us and yet there is something moving about hearing together. Even if we hear different things we are invited to reflect on the same story.

I am proposing that preaching prepares us for the work of being reconciled to one another. The reconciliation does not happen during the sermon, but the sermon equips us for renewed relationship with others. If I may draw on the anatomical metaphor, in addition to strengthening connection to the divine, preaching can strengthen the connective tissues of the body so that we are more firmly connected to each other. Preaching accomplishes this by reminding us of our shared identity in Christ through baptism, and the value of each member of the body. It can feed us a good, nurturing diet of truth-telling and gospel news that ensures the health of the body on an ongoing basis. Once truth-telling and confession have taken place, what is the homiletical task? To nurture baptismal identity and ethics; to create threads of connection; to raise awareness and understanding.

Baptismal identity is wide—there is room for diversity of opinion, identity, and behavior. In baptism, we proclaim Christ crucified and risen—actions which set us free from the powers of death and sin. In Christ, we are forgiven. The good news is that we are free to move in a new direction as baptized people. What this means for relationships is that there is a possibility of repair for harm done. Preaching maintains the possibility of forgiveness and reconciliation within the body of Christ even though those things may seem impossible. All of this is based on God's love and the way it filters into community life, animating the body of Christ. As theologian Charles Fensham writes, "Every text we read, and every discernment and judgment we make, and every way we behave towards others, be it about slavery, the role of women, or sexual behavior must be read through the refining lens of the love commandment. It is the love commandment that demands and imposes the love of God and neighbor as inseparable, that is the central moral logic of Christian faith."[9] Patrick Cheng constructs

---

9. Fensham, *Misguided Love*, 24.

a particular vision of radical love, which he contends "is a love so extreme that it dissolves our existing boundaries, whether they are boundaries that separate us from other people, that separate us from preconceived notions of sexuality and gender identity, or that separate us from God."[10] Preaching engages in this boundary-dissolving work by bring individuals into proximity to other stories that may contrast with their preconceived notions.

Preaching brings people into proximity with Christian others with whom we may not want to be face to face. Queer and non-queer people listen to the same sermon, occupy the same space, and have an opportunity to see each other in the fullness of their identities and physical beings. Imaginatively, we are brought into the same space with others who we might disagree with or truly detest. By participating in the sermon—as preacher or listener—we are introduced to the other in less threatening ways. As with other art forms like film or theater or literature, we are brought into the realm of the other and allowed to catch a glimpse of their self in the reflections of the preacher. We hear their stories and their interpretations of Scripture and in doing so we become just a little more familiar and a little more connected. Again, these are modest claims when compared to the magnitude of the brokenness. The preacher can be intentional about how they represent different perspectives on sexuality. They can be intentional about naming the challenges for people who struggle theologically and biblically with sexuality.

In this sense, preaching is a centripetal force that pulls us towards each other, it is an invitation to relationship. We remain true to our individual identities, and yet there is connection between us. We are separated by membranes of disagreement and blockages such as judgement and fear that prevent grace from flowing—and yet, for however long the sermon lasts, we are also invited to attend to the other in the sermonic space. This "bringing together" is motivated by centripetal love of the triune God. We are always pulled inwards toward the center of God's being, where we are hosted and embraced. The Trinity doesn't pull us in only

10. Cheng, *Radical Love*, loc. 114.

one direction. Like a heartbeat, we are pulled in towards the triune God then sent outward so that we can serve others. The sermonic space is an intimate space in which we are gently offered a window into the lives of others.

## HEALING WOUNDS

The division within the body of Christ can be characterized as trauma—as a wound that threatens the health of the body. One of the implications of traumatic wounding is that it can cause us to be unable to imagine a future that is different from the past and present. We can feel that we are endlessly caught in a loop of sameness—plagued by pain and suffering without being able to imagine a way out. In my book *Unspeakable: Preaching and Trauma-Informed Theology*, I suggest that preachers act as midwives of the imagination.[11] Midwives accompany pregnant people throughout the process of pregnancy, labor, delivery, and afterwards. Their job is to assist the pregnant person to create something new—a brand new life. Midwives don't do the work of creating something new—they point to what is already happening, reminding the pregnant person that at the end of the experience there will be new life. They know the history of the situation, they are trained to intervene when things go wrong, and they provide resources to support the pregnant person and their family.

Preachers act as midwives when they point consistently to God's gracious movement to bring about new life. In Scripture and in our experience, there are glimmers of hope that proclaim that the way things are is not the way things must be. This is the prophetic witness—to point to a future that has not yet arrived but is entirely rooted in God's gracious being. By pointing to examples of reconciliation and forgiveness in Scripture and in our experience, we are helping to bring about something new in the lives of our listeners. We are helping to midwife imagination—to support traumatized communities to see beyond their current situation. In

---

11. Travis, *Unspeakable*, chapter 4.

terms of the traumatic division related to sexuality, we make the audacious claim that division and hatred are not the only possibilities for the body of Christ. Instead, we are invited to see beyond division to a oneness that both preserves space for individual belief and nurtures the well-being of the entire community.

Some of the division regarding sexuality stems from a lack of understanding. At the very least, the preaching task can demystify sexuality by providing information and clarity about the issues surrounding sexuality. Sermons can begin to put biblical and theological context around sexuality, combatting misinformation. Listeners come to the experience of preaching with all kinds of erroneous beliefs and information. They make assumptions about what the Bible says and what theologians say about sexuality. By exposing listeners to sex- and body-positive theology, we are altering the conversation. In sermons, we can tell the truth about sex and sexuality in a manner that begins to unravel misinformation, so that individuals may encounter each other on a truthful footing.

We are not left alone, without resources, in this search for healing and reconciliation within the Christian community. The Holy Spirit enables us to overcome barriers and challenges that seem insurmountable. In partnership with the Spirit, preachers can provide listeners with theological tools that equip them to seek healing in their relationships. This chapter has discussed some of the parameters of reconciliation and what that might look like in the Christian community given the wounding that has taken place. The next section of this book proposes actions and postures that support reconciliation in the body of Christ. Homiletical and hermeneutical tools contribute to the healing of the broken body.

# 5

# Healing Biblical Interpretation

## DIFFICULT QUESTIONS

When I was in high school, a group of us attended a Christian youth conference. A young man in our group was wrestling with his sexual orientation. It became a group project. Was it okay to be gay? What did the church believe? What did the Bible say? There were no clear answers available to us. I can remember being joyfully convinced that my friend's wrestling was sacred, as was his eventual realization that he was indeed gay. I will not forget the delight of watching him settle into the knowledge of who he was, which was both terrifying and liberating for him. In that case, I did not need biblical wisdom to tell me what was good and holy. Later, when I turned to Scripture for confirmation, I found not very much useful information about sex and sexuality. What I did find, however, was a biblical witness that calls to the beauty of creation and delight in what God has made.

The Bible is a complex collection of sources that have been used as weapons of oppression as well as tools for liberation. Biblical arguments have supported social evils such as the oppression of women, slavery, and the suppression of sexual minorities. The

## Healing Biblical Interpretation

Bible has also been a significant source of empowerment and freedom for these same groups. It speaks to the complexity and flexibility of the biblical witness that oppression and liberation can be found in the same scriptural texts. The difference is a matter of interpretation. The interpretation of texts has played a significant role in the unfolding of debates about human sexuality, as contrasting perspectives seek confirmation in the words of Scripture. My purpose here is not to revisit the debates but to suggest a posture for interpreting texts in a manner that remembers the body and encourages the healing of wounds.

Since Scripture holds a central and sacred place in the life of the church, it makes sense that we measure our ethics and identities against the Bible. As a preacher from the Reformed tradition, I cannot have a conversation about preaching without also talking about the Bible. Preaching is an interpretation of Scripture. With what posture will we approach sacred Scriptures when we are learning to preach affirming sermons that heal the body of Christ? Phil Snider says it well:

> It's unfortunate that Christians who are open and affirming of the LGBTQ community have often been accused of not taking the Bible seriously or of rejecting the Bible altogether to assimilate to a culture that is rapidly changing its attitudes in matters related to human sexuality and gender identity . . . This popular caricature is hardly accurate. Indeed, the affirmation, welcome, and good news for LGBTQ people . . . is announced not in spite of the Bible, but because of the Bible; not in spite of one's faith, but because of one's faith; not in spite of Jesus, but precisely because of Jesus.[1]

The Bible is the source of our understanding about our own bodies and our collective body. If we are to take the Bible seriously, we will indeed find liberation for Christ's body.

Christians have often struggled with biblical notions of sexuality because certain Old Testament texts seem to say negative things about same-sex relationships. I am often asked: "Why is

---

1. Snider, *Justice Calls*, loc. 136.

God so mean in the Old Testament and so kind in the New Testament?" I usually mumble something about grace and change and God showing up in different ways. The truth is that for a long time I didn't have an adequate answer to the question. Despite my many courses in the first and second Testaments in seminary, no one had ever sufficiently bridged the gap between the two. Our perception of Scripture is that God is very different in the two Testaments. I do not believe that God changed, progressed, or improved throughout the centuries. Rather, God revealed Godself in different ways. The authors of the Old Testament were learning to see God as a monotheistic covenantal deity. The authors of the New Testament were learning to see God as revealed by Jesus Christ. As people encountered God in new ways, people wrote about their experiences of who God was and what God was doing in the world. As their experience of the divine changed, they wrote different things.

The Old Testament is the story of a people—a story that spans generations. The New Testament is written by and about a small sect of Judaism whose whole lives had shifted because of an encounter with Jesus Christ. It is no wonder that these groups had different theologies—different ways of explaining divine action and presence. The Word made flesh was present from the beginning; the same Spirit hovered over the waters. God was consistent and persistent in their relentless pursuit of humanity and human beings responded in different ways at different times in history. As we read the sacred text, we are invited to wrestle with the questions that faced the original authors and their communities. This will involve honoring the experience and perspective of those communities of faith while recognizing that as Christians we have a particular understanding of who God is and how God acts. Of course, it is vitally important that we consider the context of those communities, as well as our own various contexts in the here and now.

We come to Scripture as whole beings with histories and identities. We come with theologies and lenses that shape how we interpret what we read in Scripture. My childhood God was vaguely angry and guilt-inducing. This God was strongly male and operated the workings of the earth from a complex dashboard in heaven. This was a God who controlled, who punished, and who demanded things from me. I would feel guilt, for example, if I stayed home from church on a Sunday morning because of illness or malaise. I experienced God in this way because of what I was taught and what I absorbed from those around me. I can also see a shift in my theology as an older child, as I was introduced to the person of Jesus Christ. Jesus profoundly shifted my theology toward an understanding of a merciful, loving, and just God. In the same way, the person of Jesus Christ influences the way that believers understand God's own nature. Jesus spoke of a God who loved humanity to the point of becoming human, relentless in the pursuit of humankind. In response to this great love, people are invited to love one another just as God has loved them. This invitation is good news indeed but will seem like hard work for many of us. To love one's neighbor, no matter how different from us, or how much we disagree with them, is a gospel call. Moreover, we are called to love even our enemies, which is yet more difficult.

Another question I am asked frequently is: "But doesn't the Bible say that same sex relationships are immoral?" The Bible says a lot of things. In a comical yet meaningful exploration of biblical ethics, Jewish journalist A. J. Jacobs sets out to follow all the rules in the Bible for one year. In series of hilarious episodes and unfortunate events Jacobs concludes that it is simply not possible to live in an entirely biblical way, adhering to every tenet of biblical law, because there are so many inconsistencies.[2] As Christians, our focus is on gospel—what are the threads of good news that weave through Scripture, and how do we proclaim the principles of gospel? In other words, while specific texts are important and offer guidance, they must be interpreted within the larger context of the gospel. This is a broad interpretive principle. Bridget Rivera argues for rooting our interpretation in a spirituality of the gospel. "[We should] use the Bible as our measure as we explore the place and treatment of sexual and gender minority people in Christian communities. Should we not rather start by asking about a broader

2. Jacobs, *Year of Living Biblically*.

scriptural and gospel logic . . . before we read the proof texts? Should we not rather ensure that we are rooted in the spirituality of walking the way of the gospel with one another in our consideration of the Bible?"[3]

In other words, the gospel of Jesus Christ should guide our interpretation of texts when we are attempting to apply them to contemporary life.

Scripture is holy because it reflects the tender and fearful encounters of humanity with the divine. It is authoritative because the community of faith that spans the whole history of the church has deemed it to be so. We continue today to have encounters with the divine, and we are called to communicate what we have experienced. These experiences shape how we interpret Scripture, which in turn shapes how we view the world and God. In a reciprocal process, Scripture and experience form us as people of faith.

Preachers are invited to wrestle with their approach to Scripture. In what way is Scripture holy? In what way is it authoritative? The answers to these questions will affect how we interpret and respond to the so-called "clobber passages," for example.[4] If we believe that those words were inspired by God, what does that say about our theology, our understanding of God's identity? If we believe the clobber passages represent snapshots of a moment in history and people's interpretation of divine expectation? Are all parts of Scripture equally holy and authoritative? Does an individual pericope carry more weight and meaning than a broader reading of the text? These are challenging questions. Before you continue reading, take a moment to think through your approach to Scripture. In what way is it holy and authoritative for you? How have your personal experiences shaped your interpretation of God's identity and action? What kind of biblical interpretation provides tools and resources that enable positive preaching about human sexuality and diversity?

---

3. Fensham, *Misguided Love*, 47.

4. For example, see Genesis 19:1–28; Deuteronomy 23:13; Leviticus 18:22, 20:13; Romans 1:26–27; 1 Corinthians 6:9; 1 Timothy 1:10; 2 Peter 1:10.

## Healing Biblical Interpretation

It is important that we pay attention to the ways that texts have been used to harm the community, asking the questions: "How can this text be used to hurt me? How have texts been used as weapons?" Olive Hinnant points out that texts have been used to unite and divide people of faith.[5] The biblical canon as it exists has been contentious, and affirming preaching will pay attention especially to the ways that it has been used to divide groups within the church.[6] Biblical interpretation for preaching has the potential to harm the community, especially when sermons focus on questionable interpretations of biblical texts, or view the text literally when in fact it speaks of something more complex. For example, the word "homosexual" did not appear in Scripture until as late as 1946. "The introduction of the word homosexual to the Bible was earth-shattering. For the first time in Christian history, the Bible now said that an entire group of people known as 'homosexuals' not only existed but were also condemned."[7] Hinnant argues that once this term was introduced, Scripture became "clear" overnight about the morality of homosexuality.[8] In fact, it is not clear at all that Scripture condemns homosexual behavior or identity. "The phrase same-sex intercourse refers to a behavior. The word homosexual refers to an identity. When we talk about homosexuality, we are no longer talking about sin but about people. More specifically, we're talking about a socially constructed category used to stigmatize and pathologize human beings."[9]

Much of the human sexuality debate seems to have consisted of Christians defending their ethical position based on scriptural texts. The Bible has good news for everyone, including LGBTQ folks. Most people are aware of the clobber passages that have been used to claim that some sexualities are ungodly or sinful. I do not believe it is helpful to rely on a few isolated voices in Scripture when those voices are at odds with the larger witness of the Bible.

5. Hinnant, *God Comes Out*, 49.
6. Hinnant, *God Comes Out*, 49.
7. Rivera, *Heavy Burdens*, 47.
8. Rivera, *Heavy Burdens*, 48.
9. Rivera, *Heavy Burdens*, 48.

Moreover, it is not clear that these passages are condemning sexual minorities. There are no passages in Scripture, for example, that deal with loving, consensual, covenantal relationships between non-heterosexuals. As we shall see below, for example, the sin of Sodom and Gomorrah was likely inhospitality, not same-sex relationships.[10]

Even if the Bible were clear on sexuality, we would still need to interpret the biblical perspective in light of its historical context. The Bible has a fairly cheery view of several realities that we would now name as sinful, including slavery and the oppression of women, and yet we have found ways to navigate these interpretations for our own time. The question becomes: How will we interpret a handful of text that might claim that same-sex relationships are wrong? How will we proceed given that the Bible has nothing clear to say about LGBTQ relationships?

I believe that the Bible supports the full inclusion and affirmation of LGBTQ people. My hermeneutic lens is the life, ministry, death, and resurrection of Jesus Christ. In terms of how we determine our ethics, the teachings of Jesus Christ are central to interpreting Scripture for Christians. As Rivera has suggested, we need a broad scriptural and gospel logic. For me, that logic is rooted in the person and work of Jesus. Jesus had a high tolerance for difference and was frequently found at table even with those who did not meet the social requirements of the society at large. In Christ, we are baptized into one body. Baptism is a central practice of the church that positions us in relation to Jesus and each other. We are called beloved and named as God's own. Moreover, we are called to love our enemies. Even if Scripture was less ambiguous about LGBTQ relationships, we would be called to love our enemies. Unfortunately, within the church this has often resulted in a "love the sinner, hate the sin" mentality, or a "welcome but not affirming" attitude that claims to love the individual while denying them the right to a full and abundant life that includes sexual behavior.

Disability theologian Sarah Jean Barton defines the baptismal life as one characterized by Jesus-centeredness, participation,

---

10. Cunnington, *Open Wide the Gates*.

and community. Christians are called to become who they are through baptism.[11] That is, we are individually and communally defined by the baptized body. We are naturally drawn into an ethic of care that remembers the interdependence of the body, just as we are drawn into a community in which the primary identity is belonging-in-Christ. All parts of the body belong, none are superfluous. Our baptismal identity is in belonging-in-Christ and our ethic is to care for that body. We approach the text as members of the body of Christ. Our ethic of care assumes that we will consider the well-being of all members when we interpret the text. Our belonging-in-Christ assumes that we come to Scripture as those who are rooted in Christ through our baptism, and we approach Scripture as a baptized body.

## BIBLICAL INTERPRETATION THAT RE-MEMBERS THE BODY OF CHRIST

Biblical interpretation that honors sexual diversity should not be attempted alone. It is a communal task for the body of Christ, including a variety of voices and leaving room for the Holy Spirit to shift our entrenched positions in favor of new directions. The field of homiletics has upheld a vision for communal biblical interpretation, particularly espoused by Lucy Rose and John McClure, and more recently, Shauna Hannan.[12] I am not sure how fully these communal preaching proposals have infiltrated actual preaching practices. In my experience, preachers tend to be Lone Rangers in their preparation, their crafting, and their delivery of sermons. It is time to take seriously the task of interpreting Scripture together, in community. When it comes to preaching about human sexuality, interpretation must be shared and must include sexual diversity at the table. The simplest way to accomplish this is to include LGBTQ voices in your exegetical process, both in conversation with those around us and in conversation with a broad range of scholars.

11. Barton, *Becoming the Baptized Body*, loc. 2806.
12. See McClure, *Roundtable Pulpit*; Rose, *Sharing the Word*; Hannan, *Peoples' Sermon*.

## Remembering the Body

In my introductory preaching course, I teach a very simple form of exegesis that is designed to enter conversation with the text and the context. First, students engage in conversation *with* the text. Beyond merely reading the text, this stage involves entering deeply into the biblical text, asking questions and exploring what the text actually says. This is largely a solo task, an opportunity for the preacher to delve into the word. Outside sources are not sought at this stage, beyond definitions. An incredibly helpful resource for this stage is Anna Carter Florence's *Rehearsing Scripture*, which encourages a deep dive into the Scripture in an embodied way.[13] At this stage, the questions for interpretation might be: Has this text been used to harm LGBTQ people? How has this text been used to divide, rather than unite people?

Second, students engage in conversations *about* the text. Now is the time to seek out commentary and opinion about the text. Students are encouraged to have as many conversations with as people as possible—including written commentaries, friends, congregants, and other sources that may not immediately seem obvious—for example social media is a fabulous way to connect to others who are preaching on lectionary passages. Queer voices can easily be included in the conversation in a manner that honors their unique contribution. Ideally, preachers can set up some kind of biblical interpretation group that includes some diversity in sexual identity. At this stage, it is helpful to ask these kinds of questions: What are the range of possibilities for interpreting this passage? How do voices differ in their interpretation?

Third, students engage in conversation with their contexts. This is where interpretations meet real people. Students are asked to consider the overlapping contexts in which they exist—we exist within a broad culture that is composed of many subcultures. A particular congregation is a subculture, although it may contain within in it smaller subcultures. Some aspects of culture are shared—for example, the COVID-19 pandemic has been a crisis within the larger culture that affected local churches in specific ways. As leadership struggled to make decisions that would keep

---

13. Florence, *Rehearsing Scripture*.

people safe, there was considerable difference of opinion and even conflict. In preaching, the focus is on the local congregation. Nora Tisdale has written compellingly about how preachers might fully encounter the local context.[14] Similar to homiletic practices that ask preachers to develop a theme statement or focus/function statement for their sermons, this method asks them to consider the "promise" of a particular text in a particular location. What is God saying through this text, to these people? What divine promises are implicit or explicit in the text? These promises become the focus of the sermon, aiming to identify God's promises for that group of people. Preachers are invited to consider the ways that narratives about human sexuality function within their congregational context. What are the commitments of the congregation regarding inclusivity and affirmation? Is there a negative perception of sexuality or a positive one? What does the preacher know about the sexuality of individual listeners? All these questions will help the preacher to unpack the attitudes and behaviors of the community, leading to a deeper knowledge of the specific context to which the sermon is addressed.

This grouping of conversations leads toward the sermon and ensures that preachers are engaging deeply with both text and context. The preacher will gather more information than can be shared in a single sermon but will exit the process with a much better understanding of both text and context. This is a particular kind of biblical interpretation that, in the words of James Brownson, is "an invitation to the whole church to enter into a deeper conversation about sexual ethics in the hope that the collective imagination of the church may be deepened and widened to see the Bible in new ways, and to embrace its message more deeply in a new context."[15] This is an interpretive stance that begins a conversation rather than ending one. While the set of exegetical conversations I have described here may be helpful for preachers, it is useful to look at how queer biblical interpretation approaches Scripture texts.

---

14. See Tisdale, *Preaching as Local Theology*.
15. Brownson, *Bible, Gender, Sexuality*, 13.

## QUEER BIBLICAL HERMENEUTICS

Queer biblical hermeneutics are a broad set of reading strategies that aim to highlight the experience of LGBTQ people. In no way monolithic, these readings are expansive and include a variety of diverse perspectives and lived experiences. They resist traditional readings of texts that have marginalized LGBTQ people. These reading strategies wrestle texts back from their patriarchal, colonial, and heteronormative histories: "Queer reading strategies decolonize controlling dominant interpretations of the Bible, destabilize what is assumed as the normal or textual reading, and instead read the Bible from outsider social locations in an effort towards liberation from these oppressive interpretations."[16] They are concerned for the lives and well-being of LGBTQ communities, recognizing the intersectional nature of queer life—individuals are multi-faceted and live complex lives. Therefore, these reading strategies pay attention to the ways that gender, sexuality, economic statues, class, etc., are intertwined in the lives of queer people and in the biblical text. Playfully, with humor and attention to historical context, queer interpreters imagine stories differently, seeking to be inclusive of queer experience. Some will wonder why queer experience is given priority over the much more common heterosexual experience. In this way, queer biblical interpretation resembles liberationist perspectives on the text which offer a preferential option to the poor. In this case, priority is given to LGBTQ perspectives.

Chris Greenough posits that there are three main approaches to contemporary queer biblical interpretation—while these approaches are separated here for ease of explanation, there is considerable overlap. The first approach seeks to problematize texts about same-sex relationships in terms of linguistic and literary structures. This approach is very similar to more traditional textual criticism. Scholars examine the texts in their original languages and seek to find alternative translations. Greenough gives the example of the Greek word *arsenokoites* in 1 Corinthians 6:9–10,

---

16. Goss and West, eds., *Queer Reading of the Bible*, 14.

which is composed of two words (man and bed). So, a more accurate translation might be "manbedders." Interpreters have suggested that this passage refers to nonconsensual sexual activity between men, which could mean rape or other abuses of power and status.[17] Another lens within this approach examines the ancient contexts in which the texts were produced, especially in terms of social norms and attitudes around gender and sexuality. For example, the patriarchal norms would have shaped the ethos in detrimental ways for women and sexual minorities. Interpreters may also look for positive examples of same-sex nonsexual relationships, such as David and Jonathan and Ruth and Naomi. These relationships demonstrate love and care shared between consenting adults, regardless of whether there is a physical relationship.

The second approach involves "queering the Bible" and is more creative than the literary approach described above, engaging with the reader and the reader's context. According to reception criticism, or reader response, "The Bible moves way from being considered as a timeless text with accepted and approved significance for all eternity. Instead, it becomes part of a process in which the text is picked up by the reader who locates it in their contexts. The meaning is constructed in light of contemporary discussions."[18] The way the text is received by the individual or the community becomes more important than the actual text. One of the most helpful resources, *The Queer Bible Commentary*,[19] does not approach the text verse by verse but rather takes sections that are perceived to be relevant to the life of the commentator. Rather than seeking to answer questions, "it offers creative, innovative and empathic approaches to queer interpretation of scripture."[20] Deryn Guest has developed lesbian biblical hermeneutics, advocating for "the 4 R's"—resistance, rupture, reclamation, and re-engagement.[21] Resistance involves a reading strategy character-

---

17. Greenough, *Queer Theologies*, 104.
18. Greenough, *Queer Theologies*, 107.
19. Goss and West, eds., *Queer Bible Commentary*.
20. Greenough, *Queer Theologies*, 108.
21. Guest, *When Deborah Met Jael*, 110.

ized by suspicion, in a similar manner to feminist, womanist, and postcolonial strategies. The reader is encouraged to be suspicious of heteronormativity and patriarchal bias that are manifest in the text.[22] In terms of rupture, the goal is to destabilize the binary of homosexuality and heterosexuality as it is enforced in particular texts. Reclamation emphasizes that texts come alive in unique ways for queer readers, which allows them to explore the text in ways they have not previously been explored. Greenough argues that the exodus story is one that has been reclaimed and reinterpreted by queer communities.[23] Mona West has compared the experience of coming out to the experience of Israel's release from Egypt: "The themes of enslavement, exodus, wilderness wanderings, promised land and exile parallel the stories of queer Christians who risk the security of their closets to find wholeness in relation to God and the believing community."[24] Re-engagement is Guest's fourth strategy. This strategy claims that it is not the texts themselves that are problematic, but the ways the texts have been interpreted. Guest turns to the book of Lamentations as an expression of anger that offers a voice to those hurt by institutional religion because of their sexual orientation, identity, or expression. Like the author of Lamentations, we are "invited to share in the expression of outrage and distress" that lies at the heart of the book of Lamentations. This kind of approach to Scripture allows the reader to negotiate between their faith commitments and their commitments to their religious tradition.

The third approach is named "queer ways of telling" by Greenough and allows for a method of scriptural interpretation that is creative, original, and unique.[25] This is a playful reading of the text that "queers the text"—disturbs it, unsettles it, turns it upside-down.[26] By imaginatively retelling the text, characters are set free from their canonical roles and expectations. Mary Ann Tolbert

22. Greenough, *Queer Theologies*, 109.
23. Greenough, *Queer Theologies*, 110.
24. West, "Outsiders, Aliens, and Boundary Crossers," 73.
25. Greenough, *Queer Theologies*, 112.
26. Greenough, *Queer Theologies*, 112.

notes "how creatively and even joyously queer readers of the Bible reclaim some of its texts by destabilizing them, playing with them, laughing at them, allegorising them, tricking them."[27] Queer ways of telling do not take the Bible or themselves too seriously.

This brief sojourn into queer biblical hermeneutics attests to the slippery and unstable nature of this kind of biblical interpretation. The text, far from having a single meaning, becomes pliable and varied. These readings will come as a challenge to those of us who have been raised with a more traditional hermeneutic. As mentioned above, the preacher will need to wrestle with their own understanding of the text's authority and flexibility. What is not evident in these approaches is the movement of the Holy Spirit, which guides our interpretation as individuals and as a community. The church is called to be open to the movement of the Holy Spirit in and through the text, taking us in directions we may not have anticipated. There is a particular freedom implied in queer biblical interpretations—we are not constrained by what has been said before about this text, nor are we obligated to fixate on any particular interpretation. Rather, we may embrace and let go of interpretations, dancing with the text until it blesses us.

Queer biblical interpretation might indeed seem queer to those who are more accustomed to traditional hermeneutical principles. How might queer biblical interpretation inform the customary exegetical practices of preachers, expanding their repertoire of critical methods? In other words, what can we borrow that will inform our preaching on a regular basis? For the purposes of this book, I want to suggest a means of approaching the text that draws on queer biblical interpretation but also recognizes the significance of physical bodies and the corporate body of Christ.

## AFFIRMING BIBLICAL INTERPRETATION

There are several priorities for affirming biblical interpretation:

---

27. Tolbert, "Foreword."

1. Contextual Analysis: Understanding the historical, cultural, and social context in which biblical texts were written is crucial. This includes exploring the societal norms, roles, and attitudes towards gender and sexuality during biblical times. This contextual understanding helps in interpreting passages with a more nuanced view. We will recognize what we have in common with biblical characters and situations and recognize that our contemporary contexts are very different than biblical contexts. This includes examining the original language of the biblical texts and considering how certain terms related to gender and sexuality might have been understood in their historical context, which can provide a deeper understanding. This involves looking at how words like eunuch or phrases like *arsenokoitai* were used and understood in their original contexts.

2. Re-examining Traditional Interpretations: Questioning traditional interpretations that have been used to condemn or exclude LGBTQ individuals is part of this approach. This involves critically assessing the historical interpretations that have been used to marginalize certain groups and seeking alternative readings that affirm and include marginalized voices. Biblical passages and characters may resonate with a variety of sexual identities, not merely heterosexual. This process is even more beneficial when it considers the intersections of gender, sexuality, race, class, and other identities.

3. Inclusivity and Justice: Using a hermeneutic that prioritizes justice and inclusivity helps in understanding the overarching message of love, compassion, and acceptance in the Bible. Emphasizing themes of love, equality, and justice can be central in interpreting texts in a way that is affirming of LGBTQ individuals. As Christians, we read through the lens of Jesus Christ. Whether we are reading Old Testament or New Testament texts, we do so from a faith position that Jesus is at the center of our interpretation. This does not presume superiority of one testament over the other—we honor the voices who

spoke before Jesus was revealed. We read as those who believe that the story of God and God's people continued in Jesus Christ. It is interesting to me that so many non-affirming interpretations of clobber passages in the Old Testament ignore the grace, mercy, and peace offered by God in Jesus Christ.

4. Dialogue and Community Engagement: As noted above, biblical interpretation is a communal task. LGBTQ voices must be included in our interpretation process. Engaging in conversations and dialogues with LGBTQ individuals and communities, listening to their experiences, struggles, and interpretations of biblical texts, is crucial. This exchange can enrich the interpretative process and foster a more inclusive understanding. Of course, we will be challenged by what we hear from one another, especially when we hold different perspectives on sexuality. Careful listening is an act of hospitality that will foster the development of relationships within the body of Christ. Of course, this is a multidirectional conversation. Those who are already affirming are invited to listen carefully to those with more traditional interpretations.

5. We Read Scripture as Embodied Beings: One of my priorities for this project has been to consider the ways that our physical bodies matter for all aspects of worship. We come to Scripture in real human bodies—with needs and desires, histories, and identities. We encounter the word of God in all the particularity of this present moment in this specific body. What will it mean to read Scripture in an embodied way? It means we pay attention to visceral reactions to the words of Scripture—a gut response. We will wonder about the implications of the text for our own body and the bodies of others, as well as the body of Christ. Is there good news in the text for human bodies? What bodies are helped, and which are harmed? Whose bodies are protected, and whose are in danger? When bodies are clothed, fed, and cared for, this is gospel news.

How do these priorities work in the actual interpretation of texts? This section puts affirming biblical interpretation in conversation with more traditional interpretations of texts. One of the most well-known clobber passages occurs in Genesis 19, the story of Sodom and Gomorrah. In popular parlance this story is about homosexuality, which is perceived to be the sin that destroyed the cities. Evangelical scholar Brian Cunnington, however, has written a book that seeks to create more inclusive postures within the church.[28] He offers a compelling analysis of Genesis 19 and Abram and Lot's experience.

Abram and Lot settled in the Negev and became prosperous, but fighting among their herdsmen led them to go their separate ways (Gen 13). Lot settled near the "wicked" city of Sodom (Gen 13:13), while Abram settled in Canaan. While in Canaan, Abraham (who boasts a new name) and his wife Sarah are visited by an incognito God along with two strangers. In Genesis 18:2–8, Abraham is a model host in terms of Near Eastern expectations about hospitality.[29] The strangers have hatched a plan to destroy the cities of Sodom and Gomorrah, and Abraham is concerned because his nephew Lot lives nearby. Abraham negotiates with God to offer a measure of grace and mercy, based on the idea that the cities shouldn't be destroyed if there were even a handful of righteous people. Lo and behold, the strangers could not find even ten righteous people, "and the fate of Sodom and Gomorrah was sealed."[30]

Genesis 19 describes the scene in which Lot encounters the strangers and, according to custom, offered them hospitality for the night. The men of Sodom learned of the strangers' plan and surrounded Lot's home. Their intention was to gang rape the strangers who were being sheltered by Lot.[31] Lot could not, of course, permit such violence to fall upon the strangers who were under his care. He left the safety of his home and pleaded with the gang to leave the visitors alone, horrifically offering up his own two virgin daughters instead. As Cunnington notes, it was more important in terms of hospitality for him to protect his male guests

---

28. Cunnington, *Open Wide the Gates*.
29. Cunnington, *Open Wide the Gates*, loc. 2866.
30. Cunnington, *Open Wide the Gates*, loc. 2881.
31. Cunnington, *Open Wide the Gates*, loc. 2887.

than his female family members.[32] The gang, however, refused the offer, and threatened to do worse to Lot for being a foreigner. The gang members were hell-bent on violence, not merely seeking sexual intercourse. Lot and his family escaped, and the cities were destroyed. Lot's wife, however looked back on the scene of destruction and was turned to a pillar of salt.

Cunnington argues that traditional interpretations of this story miss the point—it is not a story about homosexual relations. When the gang encounters Lot and the strangers, they tell Lot to "bring them out so we can have sex with them (Genesis 19:5)."[33] This translation does not carry the weight of what the men of Sodom were actually demanding—violent, possessive sex that dehumanized the target. This is not the same as sexual intercourse between male partners. This passage says nothing about loving and consensual sex. Rape, nonconsensual sex, and violent sex are always wrong. As I write this, there is brutal conflict in Israel and Palestine, and reports of sexual violence which often accompanies war. Such sexual violence is more about power and humiliating the enemy than it is about any kind of relationship. Cunnington writes:

> The real sin of Sodom had far more to do with a lack of hospitality and an evil bent toward brutal violence than it did with any sexual inclinations that this unruly mob had towards Lot's visitors. The men of Sodom weren't out for sex; they were out to inflict brutal and humiliating violence. All they needed were some vulnerable victims; these visitors, who had no connections to anyone in the city, provided exactly what they needed.[34]

There is a stark contrast between Abram's hosting of the strangers, and the actions of the men of Sodom toward the strangers in their midst. The sin of Sodom was failed hospitality to the alien-outsider, not homosexual relations. Despite God's command to welcome and care for the foreigner, these men preferred brutal violence. Cunnington notes that Jesus speaks to his disciples about

32. Cunnington, *Open Wide the Gates*, loc. 2887.
33. Cunnington, *Open Wide the Gates*, loc. 2930.
34. Cunnington, *Open Wide the Gates*, loc. 2970.

the lack of hospitality they receive in various cities and compares it to Sodom.[35]

Ancient Israel was formed to be a people who had a very particular kind of relationship with God and with others—they were intended to bless, not harm, others.

> They were to operate categorically different from the nations around them, including (but not limited to) how they opened themselves up to the stranger, the alien, the foreigner, and the immigrant. They were to be a people who embodied hospitality, sought justice for the oppressed, cared for the outcast and used abundance to provide for others. The destruction of Sodom and Gomorrah functioned in the life of Israel as a story to remind them of the dangers of forgetting their calling. Abraham and Lot were held up, exemplars of hospitality, in stark contrast to the debased power mongers of Sodom and Gomorrah who viewed outsiders as objects to control and exploit.[36]

As Cunnington points out, given the function of this story to encourage hospitality to others, it is ironic that it has been used as a weapon against gay and lesbian people.[37] In fact, if I were preaching this passage, I would highlight the evil intentions of the Sodomite crowd, and the exemplary hospitality offered by Lot and Abram.[38] It is not a story about sexuality. It is a story that contrasts barbaric sexual practices such as gang rape with gentle, loving hospitality. Viewed in this way, this story functions to encourage hospitality toward others, including LGBTQ individuals. Cunnington argues that the "real sodomites" are those who deny hospitality—the passage calls the church back to the practice of hospitality.[39]

---

35. Cunnington, *Open Wide the Gates,* loc. 3057.
36. Martin, *Unclobber,* 59–60. Quoted in Cunnington, *Open Wide the Gates,* loc. 3130-8.
37. Cunnington, *Open Wide the Gates,* loc. 3193.
38. See my sermon "What's in a Name?" in chapter 7.
39. Cunnington, *Open Wide the Gates,* loc. 3200.

## Healing Biblical Interpretation

Biblical interpretation that honors the body of Christ respects the sacred realities found in Scripture—both the voice of the divine and the multitude of voices that tell stories about the divine. It is a serious task that demands caution, care, and conversation. However, it is also a playful task. Our imaginations are employed to bring biblical characters and situations to life. We consider both the ways that the text has harmed people and the ways it has supported them. At times, our familiar interpretations will be interrupted by new interpretations that will unsettle us. The biblical text is intended to unsettle us from our comfortable points of view. God's pursuit of humanity always draws us out of our comfort zone toward newness. God still speaks through the text, even when we abandon or revise traditional interpretations. Contemporary interpretations of texts are no less faithful than those which we have relied on for decades or millennia. God is still speaking, still pursuing us, still calling us to consider the various ways that the divine shows up in our world. Biblical hermeneutics for preaching that affirms will surprise us over and over again, revealing novel interpretations that we simply have not considered. This is not novelty for novelty's sake. Rather, it is faithful to approach the text with a belief that Scripture contains more than our human minds can comprehend. God gently unfolds possibilities as yet unimagined.

# 6

# Affirming Preaching: Sermons That Remember

## GOOD NEWS, BAD NEWS

Sermons are intended for the Body of Christ in a particular location. We preach to the whole body in that location—regardless of what individuals may believe about human sexuality and how they understand their own sexual identities. There will be those who are relatively comfortable with a variety of expressions of human sexuality, and there will be some who will be scandalized by any mention of the term LGBTQ. There indeed many people who remain relatively neutral—neither affirming nor condemning of varied forms of sexuality. To preach about human sexuality in all its diversity is both a prophetic and pastoral task. Even while we proclaim good news about sexuality, we will need to be aware that not all will receive it as good news. Thus, such sermons must be delivered with care and respect. In the words of Allen and Askew: "We urge progressive pastors to find a homiletical voice with which they can be prophetic and pastoral at the same time. Prophetic in the sense of taking the risk of standing up courageously in the name of God for homosexuals who have been oppressed and thus in calling for justice in the church and society. Pastoral in the sense of having compassion in the name of God for oppressors who are trapped in the very heterosexist systems that accord them privilege, trapped in that they are cheated of the ability to love and experience love from neighbor and God fully. As we preach to homosexuals the good news of God's liberation from oppression, we must at the same time offer to heterosexuals good news of liberation from being oppressors."[1]

WE PREACH TO BOTH oppressed (who may or may not be aware of their oppression) and oppressors (who will often not recognize themselves as oppressors or realize that they require liberation). We preach to those with strong opinions and those who have no idea what to believe. We preach to those who have caused tremendous harm to others because of their position within the sexuality debates, as well as those who have been harmed. Our sermons must contain good news for all of the above, which seems like a near impossible task. It may be helpful here to again consider the ways that good news sometimes initially sounds like bad news. Gospel can catch us unawares by enacting something that doesn't at first appear to be good. It is gospel news that all people are loved and valued regardless of sexual orientation, identity, or expression. That will not seem like good news for people who believe that heterosexuality is the only faithful option. It is bad news if one's entire moral compass is challenged. For some, a gospel of inclusion will feel like rejection—some will feel displaced and threatened by the inclusion of a variety of others in the body of Christ. It may feel like a threat to dearly held biblical principles—indeed, affirming interpretations of Scripture may be perceived as heretical or sacrilegious rather than gospel news. Queer individuals may also question the gospel of inclusion if it does not match the reality of their experience in the church and beyond. Many churches fly rainbow flags but have not done the deep institutional work that is required

1. Askew and Allen, *Beyond Heterosexism*, 6–7.

to be an affirming community. This deep work involves institutions taking the time to untangle the threads of gospel involved in their contexts. Preachers will also need to do this work. What is good news in this context? For whom will it sound like good news, and for whom will it sound like bad news?

Gospel will sound like bad news to those who are caught in webs of heteronormative privilege.

As Askew and Allen so clearly state, those caught in such a system will benefit from being liberated from those systems. This is true whether we are caught in the system as an oppressed person or as an oppressor. All need to be liberated from systems of radical evil.[2] Most will be unaware that they are caught in these systems and may resist the very idea that they are held captive by such systems. I view preaching as an exercise in liberation—seeking the health and wholeness of the body of Christ even as it is caught in systems that hurt and estrange us from each other. What I am describing as preaching that leads to affirmation is ultimately preaching that leads to liberation. The church needs to be liberated from homophobia/transphobia and heteronormativity. It needs to be liberated from a negative view of the body. It needs to be liberated from the oppositional, combative postures that often occur between those with different tolerances for sexual diversity.

Preachers must address this need for liberation in their sermons, which will require an honest accounting of the ways that all people need to be liberated from systems that oppress and maim. Chapter 2 focused on truth-telling and confession, which are central to the process of liberation. Also central to this process is self-examination, careful listening, and a desire to be free from systems that oppress and harm.

Progressive preachers will be enthusiastic about their subject matter but must find ways to communicate the gospel that can be heard by those with varying opinions and emotions. Rather than pushing an agenda, preaching that remembers gradually unfolds a different vision of human life characterized by beauty, connection, and creativity. Liberation is a slow process—it will take time. For

2. Smith, *Preaching as Weeping*.

those who are offended by the gospel of affirmation, good news will not descend like a dove from the sky. It will not come as a flash of lighting. It will be slow, deliberate work of noticing where our listeners are caught and giving them tools to become free. How can we support those who struggle to believe that the good news is for them too?

This kind of preaching remembers. It remembers the value and significance of the human body, it remembers the presence of the body of Christ, it reminds us of our baptismal identity as beloved children of God. Jeffrey Arthurs has written about preachers as God's "remembrancers."[3] In an age of forgetfulness, the preacher as remembrancer stirs the memory of those who follow Christ. This remembering reacquaints us with our God-given identity and inspires thankfulness and repentance, raises hope, fosters humility and wisdom, exhorts obedience, and encourages community.[4] Ormande Plater has written about remembering as an approach to understanding intercession.[5] Rather than merely looking back in time, "the Greek term anamnesis refers to breaking out of the limitations of time and space."[6] In other words, remembering pulls us forward into a new reality.

> Remembering means putting things back together and making them whole. By sewing a severed limb back onto a body, reattaching its tissues and blood vessels and muscles, a surgeon re-members the body. Restoring a separated person back into the body of Christ, reattaching all its parts, God re-members the body. People, the church, the earth, all creatures are re-membered when God puts them back together. At the heart of its meaning, intercession is our song that God may put the church and all creation back together again.[7]

---

3. Arthurs, *Preaching as Reminding*.
4. Arthurs, *Preaching as Reminding*.
5. Plater, *Intercession*, 6.
6. Plater, *Intercession*, 10.
7. Plater, *Intercession*, 10.

We come to preaching with the prayer that God will indeed reconstitute the church and creation. We preach to the whole body of Christ—wounded in various ways, vulnerable to sinfulness, paralyzed by trauma. Preaching that remembers the body is concerned with protection, hospitality, and healing.

First, it remembers the body—that is, it centers the human body as the site of divine activity and grace. Bodies matter—we are flesh and bone, and all our experiences happen in the flesh. Trauma, for example, is a bodily experience. Grace is also a bodily experience—as we taste and touch, see and are seen. Thus, affirming preaching places special priority on the protection of the physical body—concerned for the health and safety of every body within the body of Christ and beyond. Second, this kind of preaching remembers the body of Christ. In an explicitly hospitable way, preaching makes room for a variety of perspectives while maintaining a concern for the security of the most vulnerable. It claims the possibility of health and healing, drawing attention to the woundedness of the body and casting a vision of a healthy body. Third, preaching that affirms remembers our baptism and claims the possibility of healing through the baptismal waters. In the context of a conversation about human sexuality, a solid theology of baptism will help us to articulate the way parts of the body are interconnected and thus in relationship. It is the argument of this book that these relationships have been harmed by theologies of death that ignore the life-giving promises of baptism. Sermons then have a significant role, in partnership with the divine, to bring about healing among the membership. Preaching that remembers protects the body from harm, it provides hospitality, and it roots us in baptismal belonging and identity. These categories are overlapping in terms of concepts such as safety and the inclusion of all voices.

## PROTECTING THE BODY

Sermons are agents of transformation and good news, but they can also be spaces of damage and brokenness. Intentionally or unintentionally, our words can lead to harm. This section offers tools which can be used to prevent homophobia/transphobia and heteronormativity in the sermon.

Preachers cannot make everyone happy all the time. Listeners will often disagree or challenge what we have said. There will be times, however, when we cause harm to someone in preaching. This is a largely unintentional phenomenon that cannot always be avoided. Preachers simply cannot read minds and hearts—there will be times when our words trigger past trauma or deep unmet needs within the congregation. Recognizing the power of words to make or break someone's spirit, we walk on pins and needles, hoping that we can avoid causing pain but also aware that we preach to a multitude. When we become aware that we have unintentionally excluded, slandered, or hurt an individual or a group we should be quick to publicly correct ourselves and make private amends as necessary. Unfortunately, preachers will not always be aware that such harm has occurred. I believe a conversational approach to preaching enhances the possibility that sermonic harm can be addressed. If our posture in preaching is open to other voices, and if we make it clear that we are willing to be engaged about what we have said, we may encourage individuals to engage in conversation with the preacher following the sermon.

In a conversational congregational ethos, the preacher's voice becomes one among many, albeit a significant and powerful one. Moreover, conversation and consultation become part of the development of sermons as preachers begin to represent within their sermons a fuller range of perspectives. The sermon, then, is a continuation of conversations that are already happening within the congregation and beyond. This posture assists in protecting the body of Christ by ensuring that the preacher's voice does not override all others, despite the relative power and privilege that remains in the hands of the preacher. As the preacher chooses to incorporate the questions and concerns of the gathered body, a sense of trust may develop between preacher and listener because the listener knows that they have been heard.

The preacher will need to exercise caution, because truthfully there will be harmful attitudes within the congregation that should not be represented in the sermon. Conversational preaching does not necessarily mean that all voices are given equal airtime. Obviously, it is not helpful or faithful to duplicate homophobic or transphobic rhetoric in our sermons. As preachers, we ultimately decide which voices and perspectives should be included in our sermons. While we will not reiterate negative perceptions of sexuality, there must be room in the sanctuary for those who hold negative views. Inclusion means that there is room for everyone. How do we make room for everyone and still protect the body of Christ from harm? My instinct, and I am sure I am not alone, is to quash negative views of sexuality and seek to silence those voices. This is not a faithful response. A faithful response rooted in baptismal identity will see the worth and brokenness of those who gather for worship. Instead of representing exclusionary or negative perceptions in our sermons, we can make space for questioning and wondering. We can acknowledge that our own perspective is one among many. Jesus was an expert at dealing with contrasting perspectives: "You have heard it said . . . but I say to you."[8] In that way, Jesus would name and acknowledge the perspective of his conversation partners and then respectfully disagree. I tend to do this by acknowledging the perspectives that might exist in the sanctuary. For example: "Some of us have been raised with a particular view of sexuality that says our flesh is weak and unimportant. Some of us question the very idea that sexuality is a gift from God. Some of us bear shame and anger about the ways that sexuality is expressed in our culture . . . but in this particular text Jesus challenges our perceptions." By making room for these different perspectives, I am seeking to honor the individual's expressions of faith while allowing listeners to find space for themselves within the sermon. My own perspective as preacher becomes another proposal, another possibility, one that is rooted in Scripture and theology, but still subjective and subject to bias. This concept will be challenging for some preachers who are accustomed to holding tremendous privilege within the gathered community and may be reluctant to temper this privilege by making space for others. Protecting the

---

8. Matthew 5:43.

## Affirming Preaching: Sermons That Remember

body of Christ involves a willingness on behalf of the preacher to make space for even those with whom we disagree. Another way to protect the body of Christ is to examine ourselves for heteronormative privilege. Heteronormative privilege is experienced by those who are heterosexual. In short, heterosexuals do not need to deal with hate or suspicion because of their sexuality. As they go about their daily lives, they do not have to be watchful for their own safety because they tend to be safer in all situations than those who are LGBTQ. Heterosexual experiences are considered normative—for example marriage is expected between a man and a woman, queer folks are represented as "other," and sexuality is only mentioned in sermons in relation to male-female relationships or the negative presentation of LGBTQ relationships. Of course, heterosexual privilege intersects with other kinds of privilege related to gender, race, socioeconomic status, education, etc. Heteronormative privilege sneaks into our sermons in terms of how we represent reality. Most preachers, for example, draw illustrations from everyday life. If those examples are exclusively about heterosexual relationships, we are misrepresenting our contextual reality. Allen and Askew suggest that preachers undertake a review of their past sermons, asking about the degree to which those sermons exhibit heteronormative privilege. While the language of these questions is outdated, they are helpful questions for a preacher who wishes to perform a sexuality audit of their preaching. "1. Have I presented love, marriage, and sexuality implicitly and explicitly in heterosexual terms? 2. How often have gay people been used in imagery to illustrate something other than being gay? 3. Is the only time sexuality is mentioned in sermons in relation to homosexual issues (even if the stance is one against discrimination based on sexual orientation)? 4. How have I presented myself in relation to people who are homosexual, fighting for rights for them or with them? 5. Have I tokenized homosexuals in my sermons in order to make myself look more progressive on issues of gay rights?"[9] The audit serves to give preachers an idea

---

9. Askew and Allen, *Beyond Heterosexism*, 12–14.

of how they have interacted with issues of human sexuality in the past, and what options might be open to them for future sermons.

An acknowledgement of heteronormative privilege reminds us that not everyone is equally safe in the sanctuary. Some hold more power and privilege than others, and in a Christian context we have a responsibility toward those with less power and privilege. In the case of human sexuality, to protect the body, preachers must be especially alert to the needs of nondominant groups. Again, we come to the idea of safety. When in doubt, preachers should always seek to protect the interests of the most vulnerable, including sexual minorities. Preachers cannot make the sanctuary entirely safe—it is beyond our capacity. We can, however, acknowledge that some will feel unsafe, and do our best to protect the body of Christ from further harm.

## HOSPITALITY

A few years ago, I was visiting a seminary in the Pacific Northwest of the United States. On that day, the seminary happened to be celebrating the anniversary of the date that their denomination became affirming. It was a powerful service. They had taken the time to decorate, and the atmosphere was celebratory. As a visitor, I was moved by the commitment of the seminary to all its members, in all their sexual diversity. As the service proceeded toward Communion, I was struck by the realization that this was the first time that I had been at a communion table served by an openly LGBTQ presider. It was a powerful moment and I wept as I waited to receive the elements. There was a breaking open within me, a realization about what my own denomination was failing to address and recognize. There was sadness, too, because I knew that my colleagues in my denomination have been denied the opportunity to stand at the table to bless and break and share. There was also joy, at the openness of the table. If there was a place for all those other people, then there was a place for me too.

I wonder if there lurks in all of us a fear that we do not belong, that there is no place for us at the table. This is true for those who have been systematically excluded from the table despite their past presence at the baptismal font. It may also be true for those who have been doing the excluding—they may also question their own worthiness in the face of a God who appears to withhold love based on perceived sinfulness. Some of us will be afraid that if we come out as queer, or different in any way, that we will be rejected, squeezed out of our place at the table. An affirming homiletic will proclaim that there is room for everyone and that everyone belongs. This is radical hospitality. Kim-Kort offers a lovely understanding of queer hospitality as recognition and solidarity: "Queering hospitality blows the doors wide open in human interaction; it's not selective or methodical but a table overflowing. Hospitality is a continuous recognition of another's humanity, and simultaneously, it's a loving solidarity with that person. Further, it is seeing not only the humanity of the person in front of us but our own humanity, too."[10]

What does a hospitable sermon look like? A hospitable sermon will not merely represent others, it will literally make space for others. LGBTQ voices need to be included in our preaching and liturgies. These voices have long been excluded, to the detriment of the whole church. We can include their stories in their own words, or at least make a concerted effort to represent LGBTQ voices fairly. Shauna Hannan offers a view of collaborative preaching that literally includes the voices of congregants in the sermon.[11] She asks, "Whose bodies are front and center in your worship settings? Whose bodies are seen and heard? Whose bodies seem to take the lead in preaching? . . . Seeing the bodies and hearing the voices of this diverse representation connected to one of the church's quintessential practices—preaching—honors the diversity of God's beloved in more profound ways than simply saying, 'the diversity of God's beloved is honored here.'"[12] Hannan advocates for literally "passing the mic" to allow for the testimonies of individuals within

---

10. Kim-Kort, *Outside the Lines*, 49.
11. Hannan, *People's Sermon*.
12. Hannan, *People's Sermon*, 119.

the community of faith.¹³ In this way, diversity is represented in a real way, and we hear the stories of individuals in their own words and through their own bodies.

In a creative way, the sermon can help us to become acquainted with those who are different than us. This occurs through the telling of stories and the representations of people that are offered within the sermon. For example, certain of our guests may not be acquainted with LGBTQ folks or may not be aware that there are LGBTQ folks among their acquaintances. Sermons, if carefully and thoughtfully constructed, can help us to come to know a range of others with whom we don't have contact every day. This is facilitated by good storytelling and accurate representation. I believe that representing others well is one of the most challenging things we do as preachers—just like a novelist, we create portraits of people and groups, trying to represent them according to what they are, and yet always vulnerable to misrepresentations and bias. We cannot ever know the other fully, and our representations are always partial and flawed. Obviously the more we can learn about others, the more accurately we can represent them in our sermons.

We can also make space for those who struggle with diversity—perhaps by acknowledging that there are differing opinions, but always offering listeners an opportunity to find themselves somewhere in the sermon. I've already alluded to the idea that hospitality in the body of Christ looks something like self-care. The body cares for itself and each of its parts. There is room for compassion for those who are struggling, those who don't feel welcome, and those who wish to exclude others. In this space of theological debate, the body has been harmed, and each person—no matter their position on the issue—must be treated with respect and honor.

Inclusive and expansive language is another tool for affirming preaching. In his Introduction to Allen and Askew, David Buttrick notes that it is a book that will "help you learn how to modify your language to welcome a new liberation with your preaching as well

---

13. Hannan, *People's Sermon*, 123.

as your personal conversation."[14] Language that includes everyone and offers an expansive vision of God will be essential for affirming preaching. It is an act of hospitality that seeks to address each person as they would like to be addressed and ensures that all are welcomed by the language of the church. Each semester I plead with my students to use a variety of terms to describe the divine. I beg them to use language for human beings that includes everyone and says what they mean. Students rarely comprehend what I am asking them to do because it is a request to change their preferred language. There is considerable angst and debate, especially among those who have never experienced marginalization. For some reason, people are wedded to patriarchal and exclusive language. I don't know why inclusive language is so challenging. I remember my first encounter with inclusive language. I was at a Christian camp as a seventeen-year-old, newly minted leader-in-training, and we began to discuss gender-inclusive language for human beings, and I was shocked and mystified and defiant. I argued vehemently against using terms like "humankind" instead of "mankind," claiming that "everyone knew what I meant." My mentors and leaders were patient with me, and I learned why language matters so much. It hurts to be verbally excluded from a gathering in which one thinks they belong. I know now how painful it is for me in worship when non-inclusive versions of Scripture are used that refer to "men" only. I always feel left out. It was only once I had experienced being excluded because of my gender that I understood the necessity of using language that includes the people we mean to include. Choosing a more inclusive version of Scripture and using a variety of terms for God are both hospitable responses.[15] For example, it is not accurate or faithful to name God only as Father. God is indeed Father, but also Mother—described biblically using masculine and feminine imagery. You might notice throughout this book that I have chosen to use non-binary language for God, which liberates us from the binary of male and female. The divine

---

14. Buttrick, in Askew and Allen, *Beyond Heterosexism*, loc 57.

15. For example, most of the Scriptures in this book are taken from *The Inclusive Bible*.

is always wider and bigger than we can comprehend, and it is helpful to use a variety of language that allows us to reflect more fully on God's greatness.

There is a shadow side to welcoming everyone. We sometimes end up with badly behaved guests, those who have forgotten their baptismal identity and seek to cause pain and division within the community. For example, someone might insist on using the deadname of a trans person or try to set up a lesbian with a male partner. A robust theology of hospitality will need to account for the presence of these challenging guests at the table. When we host others in our home, it is our responsibility to ensure that all are welcomed and comfortable and included. The preacher sets the tone for how these conversations should unfold within the communal space. My spouse and I were invited to a good dinner party recently. It was good because the host took so much care not only to care for each guest but to facilitate relationships among guests. Wine was poured, cheese was discussed, and topics were gently introduced so that host and guests could become acquainted. We didn't have to guess how to behave because our host firmly guided us by modeling curiosity and openness. The space felt safe because someone was monitoring the health of the gathering—smoothing over any ruffled feathers, making connections, and ensuring that everyone had enough to eat and drink. Preachers monitor the health of the gathered community, paying attention to potential sites of argument or disagreement. Some of these conflicts can be addressed directly; others must be addressed indirectly. Hateful or exclusionary voices should not be permitted to address the gathering. Obviously, when hatred or ignorance rears its head in the space of worship, there will be a need for intentional healing.

## BELONGING AND IDENTITY

Baptism is a sacrament that shapes the identity of the gathered community and leads to a sense of belonging within the community. It leads to an ethic of care that impacts how we treat each other in the church. Baptism shapes how we understand ourselves, and how we understand others. As I wrote in chapter 2, there is a refrain of love that echoes throughout our lives, words uttered by God: you are my beloved child. Preaching that affirms humans regardless of sexual identity will rely heavily on the basic knowledge that we are beloved children, formed and crafted for a purpose. Preachers might struggle with proclaiming this baptismal identity on a regular basis when there are no baptisms occurring in the church in a given period. This is no longer unusual, especially for small churches that do not have many children or outreach programs. But do not wait until your congregation welcomes a new member in baptism before you preach about baptism! Baptism is always an appropriate topic for preaching. Baptismal theology can be incorporated into sermons every week.

It is good to continually remind the assembly that it takes the form of a body that must be cared for and protected. If we are reminded of our connectivity, we are more likely to think of ourselves as a body that needs each part to function in a healthy way. If being in Christ through baptism is a key aspect of our identity, it should shape our behavior and attitudes toward one another. A theology of baptism proclaims that we are dependent on one another, even though we are different from one another. This interdependence means that we must find ways to live together and support each other in our ministries. Of course, Christians throughout the ages have undermined the value of this interdependence by claiming that LGBTQ Christians do not belong to the body at all or should be excluded based on their sexuality. A baptismal ethic contrasts sharply with exclusionary attitudes and practices. It calls us to be one, to be holy, to be set apart by the triune God. It calls us to be an example to the world that unity-in-diversity is possible. Healing the divides within the baptized body becomes a priority for preaching.

## HEALING THE BODY

Preaching is a healing act and one of the ways that the church community confronts its past and imagines its future. By truth-telling and confession, the gathered community comes to terms with the pain and traumas that have bound it. By hearing and receiving the gospel, the gathered community learns to forgive and move forward. This book has assumed that preaching has a role to play in healing the divisions that have arisen during theological debates about sexuality. This kind of preaching tells the truth about the difficulty of those debates and names the harm that has been done—both to the LGBTQ community and to the entire church.

It is hard to live in a space of vehement disagreement, especially when there are few compromises available. After all, how can we compromise about human sexuality? At least for the next several years, the church is going to have to continue to live in this space of diverse opinion. While I am advocating that preaching must take sides in the sexuality debates, I am also urging gentleness and patience, so that we as preachers may provide space for those who continue to struggle with various facets of sexual diversity. What tools do we have when disagreement arises? Disagreement is often generative and thus to be welcomed. Every worship space is filled with people who have different opinions. Disagreement about sexuality, as we have seen, often comes with heightened emotion. I think churches make a mistake when they don't have a forum for theological ideas to be expressed in respectful and exploratory ways. If a sermon is one piece of an ongoing conversation in the congregation, how can we create spaces for honest dialogue among the members of the body?

When we gather for such conversation, it is helpful to be reminded of a baptismal ethic that governs our relationships with one another—the reality that we are all connected and interdependent. The body of Christ is invited to love itself just as it has been loved by God. It is an act of self-care for the body of Christ to engage in gentle and loving conversation.

On a practical note, preaching that moves toward affirmation will address sexuality directly—that is, sexuality will be named as part of human experience. That doesn't mean these sermons are necessarily about sex. For example, I preached a sermon that adapted the parable of the good Samaritan to a modern context by making the Samaritan a trans woman. This sermon referenced sexual identity, but it was not about sexual identity per se. Even saying the letters LGBTQ in a sermon can serve to draw awareness to the existence of the queer community. Sermons can also draw on examples from the queer community, like a family with two moms, or quote LGBTQ theologians and biblical scholars. Some sermons may tackle sexuality more directly by making it the central theme of the sermon—particularly sermons around Pride celebrations or as congregations seek to make decisions about their theological stances on sexuality—or preaching biblical texts that are explicitly about human sexuality. Most of our sermons will fall into the former category, rendering LGBTQ people and issues visible as part of the normative process of preaching and illustrating sermons. To create affirming spaces, we likely will need both kinds of sermons—those that tackle sexuality directly and those that incorporate sexuality more organically. A steady diet of sermons explicitly about sex may be more than most congregations can tolerate. Ideally, sexual diversity can be woven naturally through sermons so that it is seamlessly incorporated into our theological self-understanding. This kind of preaching happens over time—it's not about one sermon, but about the ways that sermons build community and identity over time.

## THE ART OF REMEMBERING

Memory is a tricky thing. It is unreliable. We know this because many of us lose our keys or phones regularly. In my earliest memory, my two-year-old self was lifted up to view my new baby brother through the hospital glass. I can remember the wires in the safety glass, and the candied lemons and oranges my mother saved for me in her cereal carton from breakfast. I wonder whether these memories are real. Is it possible that I am remembering based on what I have been told rather than what I experienced? To remember is to recall that which has been seen, known, or experienced. Sometimes we remember partially or incorrectly. Sometimes we forget altogether. I have argued throughout this book that the church has forgotten its core baptismal identity as it has wrestled with sexual ethics. The liturgy is designed to help us remember. Through song and story, the liturgy moves us through a process of remembering. Preaching itself is an act of remembering and re-membering. Through our preaching we remember God's promises that sustain past, present, and future. We also repair the broken bonds of relationship within the community.

Christian worship reminds us of our identity and purpose. It shapes and forms us into the body of the church—imperfect and vulnerable yet glorious all the same. Preaching happens within a context—not only a geographic and demographic context but also a liturgical context. The sermon is one element in a larger performance of faith. Affirming preaching does not stand alone but is knit into the movement of the worship service. Those who plan worship will benefit from remembering the diversity of the participating audience. They will benefit from remembering the absent ones. The invitation is to craft worship services that protect, provide hospitality, and nurture belonging.

Thomas Troeger calls to mind the social upheaval of the last decades, arguing that "groups that have been historically marginalized have found their voices and have insisted on the recognition of their full, God-given humanity. They have made it clear that they deserve a place at God's table with everyone else. Nothing changed instantly as they began to speak. The church did not suddenly 'step into another world' of equality and justice."[16] Preaching a positive vision for human sexuality will not cause the church to step into another world, suddenly. Rather, we are engaged in slow and painful work that may not be completed on this side of the eschaton.

This is the ongoing work of the body of Christ if it is to heal from its brokenness. Becoming affirming is a long process that does not end. It is tempting to celebrate too soon—to bring out the rainbow cake and the balloons and banners, and yet it is not ever finished. To become affirming is to open ourselves over and over to others, to recognize and honor their identities in the way they

---

16. Troeger, "Foreword," xii.

desire. To become affirming is to attend to wounds as they arise. There will be pain and discomfort because that is always the case when human beings are brought together into community. An affirming church will pay attention to small wounds before they become large. Although I caution against prematurely celebrating affirmation, it is appropriate and necessary to mark our successes along the way. There will be moments of transformation when we recognize that changes have occurred and that God is working in our midst to bring us closer to the world God has imagined for us.

Our faith is lived out in bodies—bodies that need love and care. Our sexuality is one aspect of our identity—it is not the totality of our identity. In fact, many queer people long to be seen to be something beyond just sexuality and gender.[17] There is something mysterious, unsearchable, and unknowable about human identity. Something that lies just beneath our comprehension—it is a memory of love's refrain, a memory of an identity absolutely rooted in a queer God who loves us in ways that transgress all our boundaries.

---

17. Rivera, *Heavy Burdens*, 58.

# 7

# Sermons That Affirm

THE SERMONS IN THIS chapter are imagined for the context of my seminary's weekly chapel worship. In that community, there are LGBTQ folks and folks who struggle with the inclusion of the queer community. While it is generally an affirming space, it has been affected by theological debates about the nature of faithful sexuality. There is considerable diversity in terms of ethnicity, age, and theological perspective. These sermons presuppose an audience that continues to struggle theologically and practically with sexual diversity. Each sermon illustrates some of the techniques and approaches that I have outlined in earlier chapters.

## MY HOUSE WILL BE CALLED A HOUSE OF PRAYER FOR EVERYONE

### Charles Fensham

This sermon was preached at Knox College, University of Toronto, on the first Tuesday in December, 2023. This was Charles Fensham's final service before his retirement. This sermon was historic in that it was the first time anyone has preached a sermon explicitly affirming LGBTQ people in the Knox Chapel. Fensham casts a vision for worship and community that includes everyone.

## Sermons That Affirm

Isaiah 56:1–8
*For this is what the Lord says:*
*"Maintain justice, and do what is right,*
*for soon my salvation will come,*
*and soon my deliverance will be revealed.*
*2 Blessed is the one who does this,*
*and the person that holds it fast,*
*who observes the Sabbath without profaning it,*
*and restrains his hands from practicing any evil.*

*3 "Let no foreigner who has joined himself to the Lord say:*
*'The Lord will surely exclude me from his people.'*
*Furthermore, let no eunuch say,*
*'Look! I am just a dry tree.'"*
*4 For this is what the Lord says:*

*"To the eunuchs who observe my Sabbaths,*
*who choose the things that please me,*
*and who hold fast my covenant—*
*5 to them I will give in my house and within my walls*
*a monument and a name*
*better than sons and daughters.*
*I will give them an everlasting name*
*that will not be cut off.*

*6 "Also, the foreigners who join themselves to the Lord,*
*to minister to him,*
*to love the name of the Lord to be his servants,*
*and to bless the Lord's name,*
*observing the Sabbath without profaning it,*
*and who hold fast my covenant—*
*7 these I will bring to my holy mountain,*
*and make them joyful in my house of prayer.*
*Their burnt offerings and their sacrifices*
*will rise up to be accepted on my altar;*
*for my house will be called a house of prayer*
*for everyone."*[1]

---

1. New International Standard Version.

A couple of times a week, my partner Charlie and I take an after-dinner walk from St. Jamestown to the Coffee Shop CoCo in Yorkville, Toronto. CoCo is one of the best-kept secrets of Toronto for its affordable but excellent coffee and affable Italian baristas with pictures on the wall of the many celebrities who have been there for coffee. On our way we usually pass in front of Eataly at corner of Bloor and Bay Street. Often, there is a woman with a very loud amplifier doing street preaching in front of Eataly. If she is there and she notices us walking up the street, her voice takes on a nasty judgmental tone when she rightly discerns that we are a couple who are obviously enjoying each other's company. Then she starts shouting very loudly and gleefully that God condemns sodomites, she points out that we and all sodomites are an abomination, and that this is the law of God and that we are going to hell. She is usually so loud and so obnoxious that people turn around and stare at her. At the end of the tirade, she usually bursts into singing a Christian worship song.

Contrast this public expression of rudeness, anger, and condemnation with the prophetic words of Isaiah as he speaks the words of God, "My house will be called a house of prayer for everyone." As this is probably my last sermon I share with you in the Knox College Chapel, these words are what I would like you to remember. Memorize them, cherish them, and let them enfold you in a blanket of God's love.

"My house will be called a house of prayer for everyone." The *everyone* includes you . . .

Now, these words do not fall from the sky. They came to the prophet, who some scholars call "Trito Isaiah" (Third Isaiah), because chapters 56 to 66 in Isaiah are identified as coming from a prophet who spoke after the return from exile. It must be noted that there are also newer theories about dividing Isaiah into two sections which are: (1) The announcement of judgment in chapters 1–33; and (2) in chapters 34–66 the announcement of restoration that is at hand.

However, whichever way you want to take these two theories, both agree that we are dealing in this passage in Isaiah 56 with promise and restoration. This is the promise, "My house will be called a house of prayer for everyone."

The passage we read in Chapel this afternoon comes shortly after the famous "Suffering Servant" passage in Isaiah contained in chapters 52–53. The two chapters before chapter 56 then follow with words of great hope declaring the *eternal covenant of peace*, and the *incredible compassion of God*. Jewish thinkers often think of the "suffering servant" as representing the suffering of Israel, and Christians have also identified these passages with the suffering of Christ and the promise that is to follow. Some Christian scholars have even called the whole book of Isaiah the fifth Gospel particularly because of passages like this.[2]

Whatever we call it, gospel as in "good news" is what this passage contains. The prophet brings to us a perspective that is shockingly different from the books of law. Preceding the promise of a "house of prayer for everyone," the prophet announces a great change in God's law. Whereas before strangers and eunuchs were not allowed in the temple—God's house—now they are not only welcome but they are treasured, and, astoundingly, God declares that they now have a place of honor.

What grand wide words these are! It is as if God's grace and love expands and infuses all things!

Where postexilic times in the eyes of Ezra and Nehemiah were conceived as times of exclusivism and ethnocentrism, the rejection of strangers as well as those considered unclean and unacceptable to God, this postexilic prophet announces the coming of a new reality—the reality of God's love and mercy that rolls like great hope and promise over the world.

Of course, the radical welcome is not without expectations. But note what the expectations are. They are not exclusive, based on identity, they are about all people joining in seeking a just society and working towards a society that worships, honors, and cherishes God and cares for creation and each other in the balance and rest represented in the idea of Sabbath as a just time of rest.

---

2. N. T. Wright comments on Isaiah as the fifth Gospel here: https://www.ntwrightonline.org/the-fifth-gospel-why-isaiah-matters.

*Then, God's house shall be called a house of prayer for everyone.*

It is this hope and this promise that our Bloor and Bay Street preacher misses in her understanding of her faith. Now, she comes by her views honestly. In my book *Misguided Love*, I describe in detail how so many Christians ended up hating and condemning LGBTQI+ people.[3] I describe how Christian churches and Bible translators all played a role. The book also describes how anger, torture, and violence became acceptable behaviors associated with the Christian church through the ages, including our own Reformed-Presbyterian tradition. Yet, this is what we need to hear this afternoon: This hatred and nastiness are wrong! God's house is to be a house of prayer for everyone. Not only does this passage prophesy, declare, and promise it—the Gospel writers claim that Jesus of Nazareth demonstrated it.

Think of the Samaritans, also considered an abomination in the days of Jesus. How did Jesus approach and treat Samaritans? How, in the Gospel accounts, did a Syro-Phoenician woman-outsider and a Roman centurion become examples of great faith to Jesus, instead of being cast out, condemned, and shouted at in the street? How did a woman described in the Gospel of John as being accused of adultery, while the male miscreant appears missing, become one whom Jesus cares for? It is not without reason that the eunuch is specifically mentioned in Isaiah and that Jesus again speaks kindly of eunuchs in Matthew 19, and that one of the first gentiles baptized is the Ethiopian eunuch described in Acts 8!

You see, we know today that one of the closest things that we can find in different biblical periods that can be associated with our contemporary understanding of gender diversity and sexual orientation is the first-century identity of the eunuch.[4] The prophet declares the future hope, "My house will be called a house of prayer for everyone!"

If ever you feel like an outsider or if you are told that *who you are* excludes you from God's love and acceptance, don't believe it. Isaiah announces otherwise and Jesus demonstrates differently

3. Fensham, *Misguided Love*.
4. See Kuefler, *Manly Eunuch*.

in his ministry. "My house will be called a house of prayer for everyone!"

This is the gospel, this is the good news, and this is already present in the prophetic vision of Isaiah. This is also the gospel that brings us to the Lord's Table. This Table is not my table or the table of the College or the Presbyterian Church in Canada. This Table is the Table of the Lord—and just like the house of God this Table is a place of prayer, welcome, and acceptance for everyone ... including you. Know that you are welcome, that you are loved, and, if you have been rejected or harassed for who you are, you have a special place of honor in God's house and at this table. In the name of God our loving Creator, our compassionate Redeemer, and our comforting Sustainer.

Amen.

# THE WIDENESS OF GOD'S MERCY

Sarah Travis

This sermon is intended to precede a public statement of confession regarding the treatment of LGBTQ persons by the church. In 2022, the General Assembly of the Presbyterian Church in Canada made such a confession, which it encouraged to be used liturgically in the wider church. This sermon invites people to consider the ways they show mercy and grace to neighbors despite all the reasons why it is difficult to show mercy and grace. It is the wideness of God's mercy that allows us to confess, repent, and continue our journeys forgiven, loved, and free. It assumes a variety of theological perspectives on sexuality and attempts to decenter listeners so that they can find themselves in the story in unexpected ways.

> Luke 10:25-37
> *An expert on the Law stood up to put Jesus to the test and said, "Teacher, what must I do to inherit everlasting life?" 26 Jesus answered, "What is written in the law? How do you read it?" 27 The expert on the Law replied: "You must love the Most High God with all your heart, with all your*

soul, with all your strength and with all your mind, and your neighbor as yourself." 28 Jesus said, "You have answered correctly. Do this and you'll live." 29 But the expert on the Law, seeking self-justification, pressed Jesus further: "And just who is my neighbor?" 30 Jesus replied, "There was a traveler going down from Jerusalem to Jericho, who fell prey to robbers. The traveler was beaten, stripped naked, and left half-dead. 31 A priest happened to be going down the same road; the priest saw the traveler lying beside the road, but passed by on the other side. 32 Likewise there was a Levite who came the same way; this one, too, saw the afflicted traveler and passed by on the other side. 33 "But a Samaritan, who was taking the same road, also came upon the traveler and, filled with compassion, 34 approached the traveler and dressed the wounds, pouring on oil and wine. Then the Samaritan put the wounded person on a donkey, went straight to an inn and there took care of the injured one. 35 The next day the Samaritan took out two silver pieces and gave them to the innkeeper with the request, "Look after this person, and if there is any further expense, I'll repay you on the way back." 36 "Which of these three, in your opinion, was the neighbor to the traveler who fell in with the robbers?" 37 The answer came, "The one who showed compassion." Jesus replied, "Then go and do the same."[5]

Jesus' parables were meant to change minds and hearts. He used elements of surprise and humor to invite listeners to reconsider their thoughts and beliefs and behavior. Parables are a kind of open speech that allow us to draw our own conclusions. There is a surplus of meaning, says biblical scholar Amy-Jill Levine, which is true of all good stories. Levine says "what makes the parables mysterious, or difficult, is that they challenge us to look into the hidden aspects of our own values, our own lives. They bring to the surface unasked questions, and they reveal the answers we have always known but refuse to acknowledge."[6]

---

5. Priests for Equality, *Inclusive Bible*, 2245–46.
6. Levine, *Short Stories*, 3.

While the lawyer can summarize the law, love God, and love the neighbor, his natural question is "Who is my neighbor?" This is a valid question, even though our Christian ethics will immediately prompt us to answer: "Everyone is my neighbor." And yet nations and denominations struggle with this question. In the news right now, Americans are trying to decide whether it is legal for unsheltered people to have pillows and blankets when they sleep on the street. Israel and Palestine are in geographical proximity to one another, yet could not be further apart. In Canada, we struggle to name Indigenous people as neighbors, and acknowledge our sordid history of colonialism. We Christians who know this story by heart also know the correct answer is "Everyone is my neighbor." But we don't necessarily act that way—in an ironic way we who represent different Christian traditions are united by the extreme challenge of loving our neighbors adequately. This ageless parable invites us into conversation with Jesus—to reconsider themes of neighborliness and mercy.

This parable is so familiar that it might be hard for us to hear it in a fresh way. We are accustomed, perhaps, to viewing ourselves in a particular role in the story. Everyone wants to be the Samaritan—don't we? The one worthy of praise, the one who shows mercy. The original hearers of this parable would not have wanted to be a Samaritan—there was no love lost between the Jews and the Samaritans—and it is shocking, even ridiculous that the Samaritan is the one who behaves well! For us, to be a good Samaritan is culturally honored. Yes, most of us will want to be the Samaritan in this parable. No one wants to be the robbers. Jesus tells us nothing about them—we don't know their motive; we can only guess that they were opportunists who encountered a vulnerable traveler and violently attacked.

No one wants to be the robbers. No one want to be the priest who crosses the road to avoid contact. No one wants to be the Levite who also crosses the road. These are the folks we expect will help—those who are trained in the laws of Israel, who know that showing mercy to both foreigner and neighbor is part of the deal. We don't know why they don't stop to help—Jesus doesn't give us any details. Perhaps they are in a hurry. Perhaps they simply don't have the resources to help. Perhaps they are cruel. Or perhaps they don't want to risk touching a near-dead body. They have their reasons.

The Samaritan is the hero of the story—he finds the unfortunate soul lying by the side of the road somewhere between Jerusalem and Jericho, arranges for medical care and hospitality, takes responsibility for their well-being, and does everything he can to ensure a return to health.

It is a beautiful story, really, a story of unmerited mercy and generosity.

It is tempting to view ourselves as the good Samaritan and walk away with simply with a reminder that we need to be merciful to others whether we know them or not. But I think there is more here if we are willing to listen.

This parable made me think about the limits of my mercy. It made me think about the limits of Christian mercy. In theory, there are no limits. As Jesus was trying to tell us, a key to living in the kingdom of God involves showing mercy even to those we do not know, and maybe don't even like. It might involve showing mercy to those we have been taught to despise. To show love even to our enemies. The Samaritan who showed mercy did not behave as Jesus' listeners expected—they expected nothing from a Samaritan. And yet, he is the one who chooses to enact mercy. Again, we don't know why, what motivated him to such generosity. We only know that he chose to treat the wounded traveler with compassion.

Followers of Jesus are expected to show mercy and compassion. This parable points to the ways that we fail to do so—the inclusion of the priest and the Levite in this story remind us that those who are best prepared, trained, educated to show mercy and compassion, sometimes do not. We know that Christians of all denominations are supposed to show mercy to neighbor and stranger, resident and foreigner, victim and perpetrator. But sometimes we don't show mercy. We have our reasons, don't we? We have made decisions in our own hearts, sometimes based on the doctrines of the church, that some people are more worthy of compassion and mercy than others. For example, the Christian church in most of its manifestations has failed to show mercy and compassion to the LGBTQ community. We have been more faithful to our misinterpretations of Scripture, our misinterpretations of Jesus, than we have been to our vulnerable neighbors.

My denomination, The Presbyterian Church in Canada, has gradually come to the realization that it has behaved badly. In 2022 we confessed to God and to our neighbor wrongs committed against LGBTQ communities. Confession, of course, is only a beginning—whether it leads to changes in ethics and behaviors remains to be seen.

When we confess our sins to God, we do so in full confidence that we will be heard, and that God's mercy is wide. We are invited to confess the ways that we have not been good neighbors to LGBTQ communities, the ways that we have failed to enact compassion and mercy on our siblings in Christ. We are invited to confess the times we have crossed the road or hurried past, or even hurled insults on our way by.

Perhaps this parable tells us something about the wideness of God's mercy. God's mercy extends beyond the person lying in the ditch. God's mercy extends even to the robbers. And the priest. And the Levite. God's mercy is available even to those who have failed to show mercy, those who should know better. As we make our confession, we may need to resituate ourselves in the story of the good Samaritan. Wherever we find ourselves in the story, God meets us there. Whether we are robbers or holy people who just keep walking. Whether we are the Samaritan or the person lying in the ditch, God's mercy is wide and available.

So, let us come before God and before our neighbors and make our confessions, knowing that a wealth of grace awaits us—forgiveness, and the freedom to choose how we will complete our own story. This parable calls us to repent—to change our hearts and minds. It calls us to be merciful as God has been merciful to us. It calls us to remember who we are as God's children, baptized into one body, raised to new life in Jesus Christ. God's mercy is wider than we can imagine. May that divine mercy inform the practice of our faith, as we seek to love others as we have been loved.

## WHAT'S IN A NAME?

## Sarah Travis

This sermon presumes that Genesis 19 has been traditionally misinterpreted, that the sin of Sodom was terrible inhospitality to the foreigner rather than homosexuality. Based on the biblical interpretation described in chapter 5, this sermon offers Christians an opportunity to repent of biblical misinterpretation, and instead center themselves in the life-giving host, Jesus Christ. Rife with images of communion, it is an invitation to a larger table that welcomes all.

> Genesis 19:1–8
> *The two messengers arrived at Sodom in the evening and found Lot sitting by the city gate. When he saw them, he rose to meet them, then bowed so deeply that he touched the ground, 2 saying, "Please, honorable travelers, come to your faithful one's house. Wash your feet, and refresh yourselves and spend the night. You can continue your journey in the morning." "No," they answered, "we will spend the night in the square." 3 But Lot urged them so strongly that they agreed to come to his house. Lot prepared a meal for them, baking unleavened bread, which they ate. 4 Before they had retired to the sleeping quarters, the men of Sodom surrounded the house, young and old, down to the last man in town, 5 yelling to Lot, "Where are these travelers who entered your house today? Bring them out to us, and let us 'know' them too!" 6 Lot went out before the crowd, closing the door behind him, and pleaded with them, 7 saying, "No, friends, don't do such a wicked thing. 8 Look, I have two young daughters who are virgins—take them and do whatever you want with them, but do nothing to these travelers, for they are enjoying the protection of my hospitality."*[7]

---

7. Priests for Equality, *Inclusive Bible*, 38–39.

## Sermons That Affirm

Whenever I travel, I am intrigued by the names of places I visit. I wonder why particular names were chosen. Sometimes it's obvious. Ocean Drive, or Lakeshore Boulevard, or Airport Road. Sometimes the names are purely utilitarian—like 8th Line or 47th Street. Places might be named after some person—Washington or Charlottetown. Place names can be unusual or odd sounding to those unfamiliar with their origin—in Canada we have the city of Mississauga—which is an Indigenous place name. We also have Medicine Hat and Wawa, Snafu and Happy Adventure. Americans have Bird-in-Hand, Pennsylvania and Ding-Dong, Texas. What happened in those places to produce such interesting names? There must be a history there—people had experiences that led them to choose certain names.

I must say I was surprised to discover the existence of places in the United States and Canada named after Sodom and Gomorrah. Other than being biblical, what would have commended these cities as potential place names? After all, the cities of Sodom and Gomorrah are described as wicked, without even a handful of righteous people. Traditionally, the sin of Sodom was seen to be homosexual behavior, and it is for that reason that Sodom was destroyed. That's where we get the word "sodomy." Why would anyone choose to name a place in North America after such a notorious city? Synonymous with depravity, Sodom seems like an odd choice. Perhaps they chose this name because they wanted to remember the biblical story—to avoid the same fate, to remind themselves not to be wicked. There might be other reasons.

I said that traditionally, the sin of Sodom was seen as homosexuality. However, most biblical scholars today tell a different story about what kind of sin causes Sodom to be punished.

To understand the experience of Lot's family in Genesis 19, we must go back a bit to the story of Abraham and Sarah, entertaining God and angelic beings in their backyard. As was the custom in the Near East, travelers visiting your home were customarily offered not only food and a bed, but also protection and care. It was a bit of a wild West out there—animals and thieves were dangers to those on the road. When you were in someone's home, it was their job to protect you from outside danger. We know this from the twenty-third psalm—the host prepares a table in the presence of enemies—at this table, the host keeps the guest safe from the enemies—offering hospitality and shelter from whatever harm lurks in the dark of the night.

Abraham does all these things for his holy visitors. He brings water and bread, and good rich food. He invites them to shelter from the sun in the heat of the day. It is in this ethos of hospitality that Sarah discovers that she will bear a child, prompting disbelief and laughter, as well as a hope that God could and would do it.

The men are merely stopping along the way. Their destination is Sodom. Abraham learns of the plan to destroy Sodom and Gomorrah for their wickedness. He pleads on behalf of the cities—partly because he knows that his nephew Lot and his family are nearby. Abraham extracts a commitment from God that the cities will not be destroyed if even ten righteous people dwelled there. As it turns out, ten was an optimistic number.

The angelic travelers come to Lot's home, planning to get a meal and then sleep in the town, but Lot, mirroring Abraham's actions, invites them in to stay for the night. The peace of the evening is shattered when Lot's house is surrounded by an angry gang of men—all the men of Sodom, young and old. They have heard of the visitors, and they are persistent and insistent that those under Lot's protection be released to them. The men of Sodom want to "know" these men—which is a biblical talk for having sex. But this is not about sex. It's about violence and control. It's about gang raping foreigners to dehumanize and destroy them. It's not about sex. If it were about sex the men of Sodom would have accepted Lot's horrific offer to release his two virgin daughters instead of the visitors under his protection. So, what is it about if it's not about homosexual sex?

The men of Sodom, in seeking to violate the foreigner in their midst, were committing the sin of inhospitality. They are people of Israel. They know that their calling and their covenant involves being hospitable to the most vulnerable. To widows and orphans and aliens in their midst. Their job is to welcome and protect and feed and nurture—that is what God has commanded them to do and, in this case, they are seeking to do the opposite. Abraham's hospitality, and Lot's hospitality—these are held up as positive examples of what kind of generous hosting is expected from God's children. The sin of Sodom is not homosexuality, it is inhospitality to the stranger, the other.

How often this text has been used to condemn homosexual relationships. We are invited to repent of that previous understanding and adopt a new perspective on this text. As we move toward a different interpretation, however, we are also invited to repent of the ways that we have been inhospitable to LGBTQ communities. The truth is that the Bible says nothing about loving, consensual sex between LGBTQ people. It says something about nonconsensual violent sex, which is always wrong. But nothing about mutual, caring relationships. Our interpretations of the Sodom and Gomorrah text have been inhospitable to the LGBTQ people in our midst. Our calling is to welcome and protect and feed and nurture the most vulnerable. And yet instead we have name-called and rejected. The sin is not their sexuality, the sin is our inhospitality.

We are disciples of Jesus Christ. We share a commitment to hospitality for the stranger. We share bread and wine with the understanding that the table is large and there is room enough for all. At Christ's Table, where he is host, we receive protection and generosity. All of us.

Gay or straight, no matter the shade of our skin, the ableness of our bodies, the language that we speak—all are welcome at Christ's Table. Here, we are invited to lay down our misinterpretations of Scripture and be taught a new way to enter the word of God. Here, we repent of the ways that we have failed to offer hospitality to the stranger—including our LGBTQ neighbors. Here, we receive grace that can be passed on to others—those we encounter in our church, our workplaces, our families. Here we receive forgiveness and a promise of new life.

Hospitality is a gift to our guests. As with many things, we are best poised to offer genuine hospitality when we have had the experience of being generously hosted ourselves.

Learn from Jesus—he is the ultimate host who welcomes and affirms us in all our identities—who makes space for all of us at his Table. There is blessing here, in bread and wine and companionship. There is brokenness here—sin and shame and so many mistakes. There is sharing here—you and I are sent into the world to offer the gifts we have received—great love, protection, mercy, forgiveness, and an assurance that we are free to move forward from the past and find new ways to discover God in the faces of those around us.

# Bibliography

Allen, Wes, and Alyce McKenzie. "Preaching to the Left Behind." https://pcpe.smu.edu/Preaching_to_the_Left_Behind.
Arthurs, Jeffrey D. *Preaching as Reminding: Stirring Memory in an Age of Forgetfulness*. Downers Grove, IL: InterVarsity, 2017.
Askew, Emily, and O. Wesley Allen. *Beyond Heterosexism in the Pulpit*. Kindle ed. Eugene, OR: Cascade, 2015.
Baldwin, Jennifer. *Trauma-Sensitive Theology: Thinking Theologically in the Era of Trauma*. Eugene, OR: Cascade, 2018.
Barton, Sarah Jean. *Becoming the Baptized Body: Disability and the Practice of Christian Community*. Kindle ed. Waco, TX: Baylor University Press, 2022.
*Book of Common Order of the Church of Scotland*. 2nd ed. (emended). Edinburgh: Saint Andrew, 1996.
Brown, Peter. *The Body and Society: Men, Women and Sexual Renunciation in Early Christianity*. Twentieth anniversary ed. New York: Columbia University Press, 2008.
Brownson, James V. *Bible, Gender, Sexuality: Reframing the Church's Debate on Same-Sex Relationships*. Grand Rapids: Eerdmans, 2013.
Cheng, Patrick S. *Radical Love*. Kindle ed. New York: Seabury, 2011.
Christian Reformed Church (CRC). "Service for Baptism." 2013. https://www.crcna.org/resources/church-resources/liturgical-forms/baptism-children/service-baptism-2013.
Cunnington, Brian D. *Open Wide the Gates: An Argument for Welcome, Affirmation, and Inclusion of Gay and Lesbian People in the Local Church*. Kindle ed. Eugene, OR: Wipf & Stock, 2023.
Fensham, Charles. *Misguided Love: Christians and the Rupture of LGBTQI2+ People*. Kindle ed. Georgia: Journal of Pastoral Care, 2019.
Florence, Anna Carter. *Rehearsing Scripture: Discovering God's Word in Community*. Grand Rapids: Eerdmans, 2018.
Gaines-Cirelli, Ginger. *Sacred Resistance: A Practical Guide to Christian Witness and Dissent*. Kindle ed. Nashville: Abingdon, 2018.
Goss, R., and M. West, eds. *Take Back the Word: A Queer Reading of the Bible*. Cleveland: Pilgrim, 2000.
Greenough, Chris. *Queer Theologies*. 1st ed. Milton, UK: Routledge, 2020.

# Bibliography

Guest, Deryn. *When Deborah Met Jael: Lesbian Biblical Hermeneutics.* London: SCM, 2005.

Hall, Douglas John. "The Church Beyond the Christian Religion." https://www.religion-online.org/article/the-church-beyond-the-christian-religion.

Hannan, Shauna K. *The Peoples' Sermon: Preaching as a Ministry of the Whole Congregation.* Minneapolis: Fortress, 2021.

Hartke, Austen. *Transforming: The Bible and the Lives of Transgender Christians.* 1st ed. Louisville: Westminster John Knox, 2018.

Hinnant, Olive Elaine. *God Comes Out: A Queer Homiletic.* Cleveland: Pilgrim, 2007.

Jacobs, A. J. *The Year of Living Biblically: One Man's Humble Quest to Follow the Bible as Literally as Possible.* 1st ed. New York: Simon & Schuster, 2007.

Jensen, David Hadley. *God, Desire, and a Theology of Human Sexuality.* 1st ed. Louisville: Westminster John Knox, 2013.

Kim-Kort, Mihee. *Outside the Lines: How Embracing Queerness Will Transform Your Faith.* Kindle ed. Minneapolis: Fortress, 2018.

Kinnaman, David, and Gabe Lyons. *Unchristian: What a New Generation Really Thinks about Christianity—and Why It Matters.* Grand Rapids: Baker, 2007.

Kuefler, M. *The Manly Eunuch: Masculinity, Gender Ambiguity, and Christian Ideology in Latin Antiquity.* Chicago: University of Chicago Press, 2001.

Levine, Amy-Jill. *Short Stories by Jesus: The Enigmatic Parables of a Controversial Rabbi.* Kindle ed. San Francisco: HarperOne, 2014.

Martin, Colby. *Unclobber: Rethinking Our Misuse of the Bible on Homosexuality.* 1st ed. Louisville: Westminster John Knox, 2016.

McClure, John S. *The Roundtable Pulpit: Where Leadership and Preaching Meet.* Nashville: Abingdon, 1995.

Oxford English Dictionary, s.v. "Affirm (v.)." https://doi.org/10.1093/OED/7303619905.

———. "Remember (v.1)." https://doi.org/10.1093/OED/1169664226.

Plater, Ormonde. *Intercession: A Theological and Practical Guide.* Cambridge: Cowley, 1995.

Presbyterian Church in Canada (PCC). "Book of Forms." 2024. presbyterian.ca>wp-content>uploads>2024-Book-of-forms.

———. "Confession Indigenous." 1994. https://presbyterian.ca/justice/social-action/indigenous-justice/.

———. "Confession to God and LGBTQI People." 2022. https://presbyterian.ca/2022/06/07/confession-to-god-and-lgbtqi-people/.

———. "Special Committee Re: LGBTQI Listening." Final Report of the Rainbow Communion. Don Mills, ON: 2021. https://presbyterian.ca/sexuality/listening.

Priests for Equality. *The Inclusive Bible: The First Egalitarian Translation.* Kindle ed. Lanham, MD: Rowman & Littlefield, 2007.

Rivera, Bridget Eileen. *Heavy Burdens: Seven Ways LGBTQ Christians Experience Harm in the Church.* Kindle ed. Grand Rapids: Brazos, 2021.

# Bibliography

Rose, Lucy Atkinson. *Sharing the Word: Preaching in the Roundtable Church.* 1st ed. Louisville: Westminster John Knox, 1997.

Sancken, Joni S. *All Our Griefs to Bear: Responding with Resilience after Collective Trauma.* Harrisonburg, VA: Herald, 2022.

———. *Words That Heal: Preaching Hope to Wounded Souls.* Nashville: Abingdon, 2019.

Senn, Frank C. *Embodied Liturgy: Lessons in Christian Ritual.* Minneapolis: Fortress, 2016.

Smith, Christine M. *Preaching as Weeping, Confession, and Resistance: Radical Responses to Radical Evil.* 1st ed. Louisville: Westminster John Knox, 1992.

Snider, Phil. *Justice Calls: Sermons of Welcome and Affirmation.* Kindle ed. Eugene, OR: Cascade, 2016.

Stuart, Elizabeth. "Sacramental Flesh." In *Queer Theology: Rethinking the Western Body*, edited by Gerard Loughlin, 65–75. Malden, MA: Blackwell, 2007.

Taylor, W. David O. *A Body of Praise: Understanding the Role of Our Physical Bodies in Worship.* Grand Rapids: Baker Academic, 2023. At ProQuest Ebook Central, http://ebookcentral.proquest.com/lib/utoronto/detail.action?docID=29420329.

Tisdale, Leonora Tubbs. *Preaching as Local Theology and Folk Art.* Minneapolis: Fortress, 1997.

Tolbert, A.M. "Foreword." In *Take Back the Word: A Queer Reading of the Bible*, edited by R. Goss and M. West. Cleveland: Pilgrim, 2000. At ProQuest Ebook Central, https://ebookcentral-proquest-com.myaccess.library.utoronto.ca/lib/utoronto/detail.action?docID=6110644.

Travis, Sarah. *Unspeakable: Preaching and Trauma-Informed Theology.* Eugene, OR: Cascade, 2021.

Tutu, Desmond. *No Future Without Forgiveness.* Kindle ed. New York: Doubleday, 2000.

Troeger, Thomas. "Foreword." In *God Comes Out: A Queer Homiletic*, by Olive Elaine Hinnant, xi–xiii. Cleveland: Pilgrim, 2007.

West, Mona. "Outsiders, Aliens, and Boundary Crossers: A Queer Reading of the Hebrew Exodus." In *Take Back the Word: A Queer Reading of the Bible*, edited by R. Goss and M. West. Cleveland: Pilgrim, 2000. At ProQuest Ebook Central, https://ebookcentral-proquest-com.myaccess.library.utoronto.ca/lib/utoronto/detail.action?docID=6110644.

West, Mona, and Robert Goss, eds. *Queer Bible Commentary.* 2nd ed. London: SCM, 2022.

Winner, Lauren F. *The Dangers of Christian Practice: On Wayward Gifts, Characteristic Damage, and Sin.* New Haven: Yale University Press, 2018.

www.ingramcontent.com/pod-product-compliance
Lightning Source LLC
Chambersburg PA
CBHW031501160426
43195CB00010BB/1060